TYPHUS

JEAN-PAUL SARTRE
TYPHUS

TRANSLATED
BY CHRIS TURNER

EDITED AND WITH AN INTRODUCTION
BY ARLETTE ELKAÏM-SARTRE

Seagull
BOOKS

LONDON NEW YORK CALCUTTA

Seagull Books 2010

Typhus: Scenario © Editions GALLIMARD, Paris, 2007
English translation © Chris Turner 2010
First published in English by Seagull Books, 2010
ISBN-13   978 1 9064 9 742 2

British Library Cataloguing-in-Publication Data
A catalogue record for this book is available
from the British Library

Typeset and designed by Seagull Books, Calcutta, India
Printed and bound in India by Leelabati Printers, Calcutta

CONTENTS

By mid-1943, the Pathé company had realized that, with Liberation perhaps imminent, it was possible to envisage new projects, free of restrictions. But life would not go on again as it had just before the war. And neither would the cinema. A fresh start seemed necessary. But what kind of fresh start?

The production company decided to approach writers to produce screenplays. Sartre was among those sounded out and he agreed to the idea. Meetings were held, with novelists, dramatists and young film directors, the question being: what would appeal to the public as it emerged from the disastrous years of Occupation?

Sartre had his opinion on this and expressed it in the underground press. The cinema should make people think, at the same time as it entertained and moved them. It alone had the power to do this, and to do it for the broad mass of the people. He felt that, with the coming of the 'talkies', the seventh art's evocative power had been forgotten—the broadening of horizons of which it was capable, and which the great silent directors had exploited so astutely. 'This giant has been forced to paint miniatures,' he wrote. Sartre dreamed of modern equivalents of *Metropolis* and *Birth of a Nation*, which would make viewers fully aware that they existed not only as individuals, but also as collective beings. It was necessary, 'to speak to crowds of crowds'. They too have their passions, their hopes and disillusionments, their heroism or their cruelty, their tragic infatuations. 'This does not mean cinema must deny itself romantic dramas or conflict between individuals . . . The speed with which the camera can fly from place to place enables us, moreover, to situate our story in the entire universe.'[1] We may note in passing that *The Reprieve*, the second of the trilogy of novels Sartre was writing at this same time, attempted—though, in that case, using words—to convey a sense of collective anxiety, as threats of war loomed in the week before the Munich agreement.

Of the synopses, fleshed-out to varying degrees, which Sartre submitted to the company's readers in the ensuing months, *Les jeux sont faits* and *Typhus* were seen by Jean Delannoy as being of interest. The former was eventually judged 'too metaphysical' by the Pathé management and, for the moment, Delannoy gave up the idea of making it.[2] The producers were more seriously interested in *Typhus*. Sartre had drafted a 70-page treatment, presumably in narrative form.[3] He was assigned the screenwriter Nino Frank as technical adviser and worked with him during the winter of 1943–44.[4] Guided by the criticism and suggestions of a professional, he reshaped his text into broad sequences with precise visual and auditory directions that speak to the imagination. It is this script we publish here, in the quasi-professional form in which it was presented, following the manuscript held at the Bibliothèque nationale in Paris.

Sartre had reason to hope that, after some tighter editing, it might be filmed more or less as he had conceived it. In the event, various reservations emerged. One of the first sequences ('the dead body on the bus roof') which had, on a first reading, seemed admirable, was regarded upon mature reflection as too shocking and, moreover, impossible to film. The role of the heroine—a cabaret singer on the verge of sliding into prostitution—did not suit the actress who had been approached to play the part. It is also possible that the story itself, which Sartre situated in Malaysia under the British protectorate, may have put the producers off for material or political reasons.

Sartre would no doubt have had to make the time to defend his screenplay, to discuss the prospective reworkings in great detail. The writer's labour is a solitary activity; it did not predispose him to prolonged dialogue. And he now had less and less time. Apart from the writing of *The Reprieve*—which he was itching to get back to, after setting it aside to work on *Typhus* and write *Huis Clos* (In Camera)—he was secretly preparing, with Maurice Merleau-Ponty, to launch the political and literary magazine that would become *Les*

Temps modernes, another project for the post-war period. In March 1945, the press announced that filming would begin on *Typhus* shortly. But in the January Sartre had flown to the USA as part of a press mission. He had been keen to see his screenplay filmed, but he ended up handing the project over entirely to Delannoy, who did not go ahead with it.

Some years later, Yves Allégret made *Les Orgueilleux* (The Proud Ones) with Michèle Morgan and Gérard Philipe. The plot was in part inspired by *Typhus*, but it no longer involved a singer whose career was on the slide nor, more significantly, an epidemic in the colonies. Only one scene, the 'bear dance' performed by Gérard Philippe, seems to us to resemble Sartre's scenario. Allégret's film came out in 1953, with Sartre resolutely denying paternity.[5]

A. Elkaïm-Sartre

2007

Notes

1 These words are from an unsigned article by Sartre, 'Un film pour l'après-guerre' (*L'Écran français*, issued as a section of the clandestinely published *Lettres françaises*, 15 April 1944).

2 See Jean Delannoy, *Aux yeux du souvenir* [In the Eyes of Memory] (Paris: Les Belles Lettres, 1998). He later succeeded in convincing another producer to take up *Les jeux sont faits* and the film (English title: *The Chips are Down*) was released in 1947.

3 See *Lettres au castor et à quelques autres, tome 2, été 1943* [Letters to the Beaver and to Some Others] (Paris: Gallimard, 1983).

4 See Nino Frank, *Petit cinéma sentimental* (Paris: La Nouvelle Édition, 1950).

5 The screenplay of *Les Orgueilleux* [The Proud Ones] is clearly attributed to Jean Aurenche, but the DVD issued by Éditions René Chateau in 2004 bears on its cover the words: 'd'après un scénario de Jean-Paul Sartre'. [Trans.]

TYPHUS

View of a deserted street. Little, low mud-built houses. The camera moves down the street. All the doors are open, giving on to dark, empty rooms. The camera closes in on one of the small houses, the door of which seems closed. The door is flung open from the inside, right back against the wall. A dog runs howling from the house.

A dog barking. This sets off others which answer it from various parts of the town.

A reed-covered market. The sun shines through the reeds and vines, leaving patches of sunlight on the ground. The camera moves forward beneath the canopy. The ground is strewn with fruit. A jumble of fabrics on a stall.

Another stall with a pyramid of prickly pears. The scrawniest of cats walks across the stall and behind the fruit. The pyramid collapses. The fruits fall off the stall and roll on to the ground. We follow one of the pears that rolls into the corner of a stall half in darkness. Right beside where it comes to a halt, there is a still, bare foot.

Dogs bark further off in the distance.

The barking dog recedes into the distance and is heard only in the background.

Shot of the bare foot.

Deathly silence.

Immediately after, shot of a skinned, dead sheep hanging up on a butcher's deserted stall.

Silence.

3

A pack of bony dogs crosses the alley. The sun on their skinny backs. One of them stops in front of the dead sheep. He tries to jump up on the stall and falls back down. The other dogs come to a halt too. They begin to growl.

A new European-style street. Many shops with their steel shutters down: *Frisco Tailors, the Zanzi-Bar, Bookshop-Stationers*. The signs of the defunct shops parade slowly before us.

Deathly silence.

In the middle of the carriageway are tram rails. On the rails, an empty, abandoned tramway trailer. The sun beats down oppressively. At the end of the street is a large square (similar to the Place Djema'a el-Fna in Marrakesh). Pottery piled up. In another place, a heap of empty tins and, in yet another, a tent. A native, dressed only in a loin-cloth is lying with his arms out-stretched. We come closer to him.

Sound of an engine idling.

Close-up: the native's head, his eyes staring blankly, his mouth half-open. An enormous fly is walking across his upper lip. A swarm of flies above his

Engine noise.

head. One of them settles on the white of one of his eyes. The camera moves back and the field widens. View of the square: the pottery, the dead Malay and, at the other end, outside a European hotel, there stands a bus. The camera takes this all in in a single shot.

The bus seen from the side (the camera is on the pavement beside where the bus is parked). On the roof of the bus, trunks and mattresses, a bicycle, suitcases and a pram. A ladder has been leaned against the bus.

Engine noise. Dogs barking in the distance.

The inside of the bus, shot aslant, from the driver's seat. Beside the driver, two empty seats. Behind him, some 20 persons, Whites only, men, women and children, tightly packed and silent.

View of a hand drumming on the back of a seat.

Engine noise.

The camera moves down towards the back of the bus. We see the faces, row by row.

First row on the right: an old, white-haired man, of noble appearance like Richard Wagner; clean-shaven, in a velvet cap and floppy necktie. Beside him, his wife in a black hat. She is thin and has a lean, cantankerous face.

Last row on the left: two rather pretty women in their thirties with children. A 10-year-old boy standing between their legs, a little girl of six sitting on her mother's knee (the first woman to the left of the aisle), a 10-month-old baby in the other woman's arms. The two women, still and pale, staring straight ahead.

Second row on the right: a shrewd-looking, round-faced old woman with enormous parcels on her knees. Two twin sisters at an awkward age (their hair in plaits), sharing a single seat.

On the left: a tall, thin man with a moustache; beside him, a portly, bearded man, nervously chewing at his beard.

Etc.

Shot of a foot (man's shoe) impatiently tapping on the floor at regular intervals.

Shot of the portly, bearded man nibbling at his moustache. Shot of the hand drumming on the back of the seat.

Sound of dull, regular tapping, against the *basso continuo* of the engine.

The tapping, muffled at first, increases in intensity. Grave, sombre music to the rhythm of the tapping.

View from the back of the bus of the two empty front seats and of the back of the driver's neck (an enormous neck sunk between his shoulders and cap).

The same music.

The 10-year-old boy standing between his mother's knees—the two seen from the waist up.

BOY: Mummy, when are we going to set off?

MOTHER: Shhh, dear, we're waiting for someone.

View of the two empty seats and the driver's neck.
The back of the motionless driver's neck.

The old man—head and shoulders—leaning forward.

VOICE OF OLD MAN: Yes, are you going to keep us waiting much longer, driver?

OLD MAN (*insistently*): You don't seem to realize that every minute counts. Our only chance is to leave right away. We should already be 60 miles from here.

The driver's back. He shrugs his heavy shoulders. The old woman is visible, looking tiny in the rear-view mirror.

The rear-view mirror in the foreground. The old lady seen talking in the rear-view mirror. Her head raised very high.

Driver's back. The two empty seats. The driver raises his left arm and shows his wristwatch without turning around.

OLD LADY: If there are people mad enough to be late in circumstances like these, we should just leave them behind.

DRIVER (*grumpily*): Five to nine. Nobody's late. We'll leave at nine.

One of the twins (head and shoulders) looks at her watch. Shot of the arm and the watch: it shows ten to nine.

The other twin looks at her watch. Shot of the arm and the watch: the watch shows two minutes to nine.

The bearded man pulls a large turnip watch from his waistcoat pocket. It shows five past nine. He sighs and adjusts it.

Shot of the two twins adjusting their watches. One of them sighs.

GIRL (*through gritted teeth*): Five more minutes.

At the back of the bus, a woman has turned around. She is looking through the back window. We see her down to the waist, almost from behind. Through the window, we can see the deserted square. Then, far in the distance, two human beings come into view running.

WOMAN (*nervously, almost shouting*): There they are! There they are!

Shot from the driver's seat: we see all heads turning to the back.

The hand that was drumming stops suddenly in the air above the seat arm.

In the street. Shot of Tom and Nellie running (front, full-length view, in the foreground). Tom, once a good looker, is now fat and flabby. Forty-five years old. Something casual about his dress: shirt none too clean and a little crumpled. He has a suitcase and a bird cage in his left hand. He wipes his brow with his right as he runs.

Shot of Tom running (alone, head and shoulders).

TOM: The engine's running, Nellie, I can hear it. The bastards, I bet they're going to leave without us.

(*Shouting*): Wait for us! Wait for us, damn you!

He waves his handkerchief as he runs along, breathing heavily.

Nellie and Tom face to camera and full-length.

Nellie gets ahead of Tom. She is wearing a white suit and a white, wide-brimmed hat. She is quite attractive, but, though young, she already has a rather jaded look. The first wrinkles, a slack mouth, a hard, seen-it-all-before attitude.

In the bus. Shot from the driver's seat. All heads are turned towards the back window. A woman with her face glued to the window as before. Through the window, beside her head, we see Nellie and Tom rushing along.

WOMAN: Hold on, I know those two!

She turns round, very animated, to the others.

Shot of the heads turned towards her, seen from the back of the bus.
Disapproving gazes from the twins and a scandalized smile from the old woman.

The tall man with the moustache (seen in the far background).

They had an act at the Canary Club.

Scandalized whispers and sotto voce remarks: 'An act at the Canary Club!'

MAN WITH MOUSTACHE (*contemptuously*): Oh, it's them. I thought they'd gone. Well, they're not even talented. Total third-raters!

Nellie and Tom full-length, from behind, running in the mid-distance. In the far distance, on the right, a Malay hiding at a street corner is watching them. On the left, the bus.

Tom and Nellie run past the Malay who watches them. The Malay alone, seen from the waist up, thin and sickly. His features are drawn and his burning eyes stare after them.

The bus shot from the outside, from the back. In the foreground Tom, seen from behind, running; in the far distance, Nellie, who has got ahead of him, getting on to the bus.

Whispers down the bus: 'An act at the Canary Club . . . they're not even talented . . . total third-raters.'

The inside of the bus: the back of the driver's neck, the two empty seats, the door. Nellie gets on, stooping to pass through the door.

NELLIE (*out of breath*): Wait just one minute. My husband's behind me. He's carrying a case.

The old lady and the noble-looking gentleman. From the waist up.

OLD LADY (*softly*): Her husband! (*She sniggers.*)

Nellie sitting next to the driver, shot from behind. She turns around and gives the old lady a cold, hard stare.

Nellie and the old lady shot from the side, on the right (as though through the bus window). They look at each other. The old lady turns away and purses her lips.

The engine.

The bus door from the inside. Tom appears. We see his head and shoulders and his right hand holding out the birdcage.

TOM: Nellie, take Kiki off me.

Nellie leans over the empty seat and takes the birdcage. Tom puts his suitcase down on the bus floor and clambers up into the vehicle.

Tom, standing in the bus, sweating and breathing heavily. He mops his brow with a handkerchief. He turns towards

Phew! Good day, ladies and gentlemen.

the back of the bus (facing the camera) and gives everyone a smile.

The interior of the bus, shot from the front. In the foreground, the old lady and the noble gentleman, etc. Stern faces. No reply.

The 10-year-old BOY, between his mother's knees (shot from the waist up). He turns to Tom. His mother gives him a little smack on the head.

The old gentleman with the noble, unpleasant manner (head and shoulders).

Tom, standing in front of the seat and facing the back of the bus (shot from the back of the bus; in the foreground, the heads of the twins and the round-faced old woman, seen from behind. Beyond that, the heads of the old man and his wife. Beyond these, Tom seen from the waist up).

Tom stoops, picks up the cage and hangs it from a net on the right.

View of a hand drumming on the arm of a seat.

View of the cage in the foreground, with the panic-stricken bird (canary)

BOY: Hello. You're late!

MOTHER: Shhh. Will you be quiet?

OLD GENTLEMAN: Is that it, then? Are we waiting for anyone else or can we go?

fluttering about and chirruping.

The driver and Nellie (from behind), medium shot. The driver stands up awkwardly.

He goes past Tom, who is standing by the door and moves aside to let him pass, and he leaves the bus.

Shot of the Malay, lurking on the street corner, looking on, wild-eyed, at the bus.

Shot of the bus from outside. The driver seen full-length by the ladder. The Malay jumps out.

The driver and the ladder (full-length, by the pavement). The Malay springs forward, grabs the ladder and rapidly clambers up it.

View from the roof of the bus, shot from below. The Malay standing on the bus roof. He stoops and disappears behind the pram.

The driver by the ladder, head in the air, stunned. He grabs the ladder by its sides and shakes it.

The chirruping of the bird.

DRIVER: We're leaving! I'm going to take the ladder down.

Hey, you . . . hey, you . . . what's this?

Are you going to come down? I said, are you coming down? Or do I have to come up there?

The inside of the bus (shot as though from the bonnet, through the windscreen).

Foreground: Nellie and Tom. Heads are moving behind them, with people leaning out of the windows.

'What is it?'
'What's happened?'
'It's a Malay.'
'He's on the roof?'
'Yes, lady. Oh, but they'll get him down!'

The bearded man, leaning towards the window.

The woman at the back of the bus, in shrill tones, almost hysterical.

The driver, outside, full-length. He is still holding the rungs of the ladder. He hesitates.

The driver puts his foot on the first rung. Nellie appears at the bus door.

BEARDED MAN: Yes, yes. Get him down! Get him down!

WOMAN: Get him down, he's going to contaminate the lot of us!

Shouts from inside the bus, which we hear through the open windows: 'Get him down!'

NELLIE: Oh, leave him where he is. Give him a chance. If we abandon him, he's done for.

The driver, motionless, his foot on the first rung. He hesitates, looks first at Nellie, then up to the bus roof.

The interior of the bus, shot from the side, as if through a window. We see Nellie and Tom, the old lady and the old gentleman.

Nellie turns round to her.

OLD LADY: This is pure madness!
NELLIE: Sorry?
OLD LADY (curtly): All the natives are sick . . . young, young . . . er . . . lady

On Nellie.

On the old lady.

Shot of the four. The old gentleman speaks with nobility and gravity.

Shot of the old gentleman alone (head and shoulders). He suddenly has a judge's cap on his head.

Shot of Nellie, who looks despairing.

The woman at the back of the bus in a positive fit of hysterics (medium shot).

Shot of Nellie from the back of the bus. She is now standing.

(*with intentional stress on the word 'lady'*). What's the point of leaving town if we take one of them with us?

NELLIE: So you know he'll die if we leave him here and you want to leave without him! Aren't you afraid that might occasionally keep you from sleeping?

OLD LADY (*with great dignity*): I never sleep, young lady.

OLD GENTLEMAN: Typhus is spread by lice, young lady; and this native is bound to be full of lice.

There are 20 Europeans here, including three children. Are you going to run the risk of infecting 20 people to save one?

NELLIE: But he's on the roof. We shan't have any contact with him.

WOMAN: Yes, and our cases are on the roof too, and my bicycle, and a pram. The lice will get into them and go everywhere—in our clothes, our underwear, everywhere, everywhere!

NELLIE: The cases are closed. How are they supposed to get in?

The bus roof. Shot from above. The native is crouching between a trunk and the pram; he is breathing heavily and seems panicky.

The driver (full-length) standing by the ladder.

Nellie gets out of the bus and walks over to the driver.

Tom leans out of the door (shot of Tom, Nellie and the driver).

DRIVER: Hey, you up there. Will you get down?

NELLIE (*softly*): Please.

TOM (*in hushed tones*): Come on Nellie, what has this got to do with us? Let the little shrimp fall off, won't you, or we'll have the whole of the bus on our backs.

The old gentleman and the old lady appear in the bus window.

The driver (from the waist up), looking up to the window.

Nellie comes over to him and puts her hand on his arm.

Nellie, smiling.

The driver.

OLD GENTLEMAN: Driver, I insist that you . . .

DRIVER: Hey, that's enough. I'm not taking orders from anyone!

NELLIE: Please.

DRIVER: I get it. On the bus with you! I'm taking the ladder down and we're leaving!

The bus from the side. Nellie gets back on the bus. The driver throws aside the ladder, which falls on the pavement, and gets back on the bus.

In the bus, shot of the driver, in the foreground, from the side: he puts the bus into first gear.

Roar of the engine.

The 10-year-old boy and his mother, long shot.

THE BOY: We're going, Mum, we're going!

MOTHER: Yes, we're going!

Shot of the tall man with the moustache and the bearded gentleman. The bearded man has the whole of his beard in his mouth and is chewing it nervously.

TALL MAN WITH MOUSTACHE: We're going! At last! At last, we're going!

He takes the beard out of his mouth and gives a wide smile.

The boy and his mother.

THE BOY: Does it take long to get to Ottawee?

MOTHER: Oh, a very long time, dear. It's 12 hours across the desert . . .

Shot of square and bus (from above). The bus starts off slowly and turns into the main street. We see it disappear.

Engine roars.

Shot of ladder on the pavement. The camera begins to move again, as at the beginning. It slowly crosses the square towards the corpse of the Malay. Shot of corpse from above. Flies on his face.

Engine noise fades.
Silence.

Distant barking, coming nearer.
Very fierce barking.

Dissolve

*   *

The Ottawee docks. The *São Paolo* is at the quayside. Shot from above of the native crowd loading the ship. Malays, carrying bundles on their shoulders, climbing the gangplank from the quay to the ship. A few Whites dressed in white linen. Intense activity. The camera comes down slowly into the midst of the crowd. A European overseer in white linen jacket and trousers beside a pile of enormous bundles. A native passes close by, walking limply and lazily in linen jacket and shorts, his legs and feet bare. We see him from behind. The overseer is watching him.

Ship's sirens against a continuous, shrill sound of native voices. Overseers' whistles.

The native carries on walking without turning around. The overseer takes a step forward and grabs him by the arm.

OVERSEER: Hey, you, slacker!

Hey, I'm talking to you. Take these bundles and put them on board.

The native turns around. It is George. He is unshaven and bleary-eyed. He seems both distant and malicious.

GEORGE: Shut it! I'm not a Malay. And I don't work for you.

The overseer shrugs his shoulders.

OVERSEER: Oh, it's you. Well, you might as well work for us. There's no shame in that, and it'd be better than spending your days prowling round the port and getting plastered. And if you're not a native, why do you dress as a Malay?

GEORGE: 'Cos I don't like Whites.

He turns round and goes on his way. The camera follows him, from behind, showing him full-length. He goes into a dark, uphill alley. Malays streaming up and down the alley; a car tries with difficulty to make its way forward, hooting its horn. George climbs the hill, cutting through the crowd. He passes a police station. A uniformed giant is standing outside. Shot of George in profile. He snorts and delivers an enormous stream of spit between the policeman's feet. The officer remains impassive (medium shot, from the waist up, in profile, head up, motionless).

The police station, with the officer standing to attention. George moving off slowly. A tall, tough-looking man comes out of the station and glances at George, hesitates a moment and sets off after him.

Full-length, front view of George. He is walking towards the camera with the inspector behind him. The inspector is taller by a head.

Side view of George. He stops outside a seedy-looking bar. The door, which has frosted glass windows, is closed. Above the door, a single word: 'Bar'.

The inspector puts a hand on his shoulder. George jumps, then gathers himself and turns slowly towards the inspector.

Oh! It's you, Inspector!

INSPECTOR: You want to go in?

GEORGE: I haven't a red cent.

INSPECTOR: I'm buying.

George looks him up and down without replying.

He hesitates, then makes up his mind.

Come on, you can spare five minutes, can't you?

GEORGE: You know very well I can *always* spare five minutes.

George and the inspector, seen from behind, outside the bar. The inspector pushes the door open and goes in. George follows him.

The interior of the building. Semi-darkness, music. We see the far end of the establishment; a small band of native musicians, a door and four

Native music, slow and heady.

cubicles to the right. Two are empty. In the third, a sailor is embracing a Malayan girl, laughing. The inspector moves towards the fourth cubicle. George follows him and they sit down without speaking. A waiter walks across from the left and comes over to the cubicle where the inspector and George are sitting opposite each other at a little round table. He stands in front of them, ready to take their order.

INSPECTOR: A neat whisky.

WAITER: And for you, sir?

INSPECTOR: We'll see about that in a minute, if he's a good boy.

The inspector winks.

The waiter turns around and goes back across the room. George and the inspector stare at each other in silence.

George in the foreground, with a distant look in his eyes, his head swaying from side to side.

Medium shot of the inspector. He lights a pipe.

Well, George. We don't see you any more. You used to come and see me. I don't like it when you don't.

GEORGE: Well, I don't like it when *you* do.

The waiter comes back with a bottle of whisky and a glass on a tray. He serves the inspector and puts the bottle back on the tray. As he is about to leave, the inspector reaches out his hand, takes the bottle and puts it on the table.

A silence. George, medium shot, looks at the bottle. In the end, he reaches out his hand to pick it up. The inspector picks it up and takes it out of his reach.

INSPECTOR: That's fine. Leave us the bottle and skedaddle.

George, whatever are you thinking of? Drinking straight out of the bottle like a Malay! In a moment you can drink out of a real glass, like everyone else. But you're not in a hurry, eh? You don't mind if we chat a bit first?

George shrugs his shoulders. The inspector toys with the bottle, while George stares after it blankly.

How long is it since you had a whisky, George?

GEORGE: Don't come that old trick with me. They do it with cigarettes too. They wave 'em under the nose of the man they're trying to get to talk.

On the inspector.

INSPECTOR: That's not fair, George. I've never refused you a whisky. Only this March you came and gave me a bit of information. Only a snippet, but you went off with your three bottles, you old sod!

On the two of them. The inspector slaps him on the shoulder.

On the two of them. The inspector sniggers.

On George. He is breathing with difficulty. He never takes his eyes off the whisky.

On George. His face hardens as the inspector speaks to him.

On the two men.

On the inspector. He directs a hard-faced smile at George.

GEORGE: Don't touch me! I might be a sod, all right, but I'm not *your* old sod.

INSPECTOR: As you wish, George. The main thing for me, you know, is that you're a sod.

Well, you see. Aren't we gonna just get along nicely? It so happens that I need a bit of information. I said to myself this morning, George is just the man. He knows everybody.

GEORGE: No.

INSPECTOR (*surprised*): What do you mean, no?

GEORGE: It's over. I've had enough.

INSPECTOR: Why's that, then?

GEORGE: I've gone off the idea of squealing on down-and-outs who've stolen three cans of food or a box of soap. It wouldn't be so bad if it was Whites. But it's Malays I give you. People like me.

INSPECTOR: What do you expect, old pal? You shouldn't have started. It's

The two men. George slumped on the table in disgust.

On the inspector.

your job now. Got to keep it up. You've made your choice. You're with us, not them.

GEORGE: Being with you makes me sick. With Whites. And with cops into the bargain.

INSPECTOR: Ah, life isn't a bowl of cherries. Now, Jim comes out of the nick on Thursday. Suppose I get him to come to my office. Suppose I tell him—just to put him straight, you see—that you left my office with two bottles of whisky the very day he went to prison. Don't you think he might give you a hard time?

On the two men. George picks up the bottle and pulls it towards him. The inspector lets him. George strokes the bottle distractedly with his hand. A pause.
On the inspector.

GEORGE: What do you want to know?

INSPECTOR: Whether perhaps you've got some pals who've told you about these bales of rice? You know, the ones that were supposed to go on the *São Paolo* and that seem to be missing.

GEORGE: Get me a glass.

On the two men.

INSPECTOR (*laughing*): What do you want a glass for? Can't you drink out of the bottle?

George shrugs his shoulders. He takes the bottle and drinks straight from it. On George while he is drinking.

On the two men: with a snigger, the inspector watches George drinking from the bottle. George notices and stops drinking. He looks up at the inspector, holding the bottle by the neck.

GEORGE: You're laughing, eh? You're thinking, I've got that old sod George where I want him. And why do you think you've got me? Because I like whisky and I'm a coward?

INSPECTOR: Well, wouldn't I be a little bit right?

GEORGE: In a way. But the main thing is that I like to disgust myself. Oh, I know. No good asking you to understand that. It's just a luxury I afford myself.

George in the foreground.
On the two men. The inspector makes a vague gesture.

He picks up the bottle again and drinks straight from it. He finishes it off, puts it down, rests his elbows on the table, and says:

So, you want to know about the bales of rice? I'm going to make you a gift of a Malay family. It's not my day. There aren't any Whites involved.

Dissolve.

*   *

A rocky desert. Shot from above. A road barely traced out in the middle of the desert. The—tiny—bus appears in the distance and comes nearer.

Shot of the roof of the moving bus just below the camera position. The Malay crouching on the roof. He looks up to the camera. He seems ill.

Inside the bus. Shot from the front, looking to the back. In the foreground, the old gentleman and his wife. The old gentleman is sleeping, open-mouthed. His wife is sitting bolt upright, staring out. From time to time, the old man's head rolls on to his wife's shoulder and she pushes him away with her shoulder.

Behind them, the old lady with the subtle smile fans herself. Several times, the twins yawn together.

Side view of the left-hand rows. The 10-year-old boy has sat down at his mother's feet. The other young woman is breast-feeding her baby. Behind her, the bearded man is in his shirtsleeves. Braces. Big, hairy arms protruding from short sleeves. His nose and eyes are in a patch of sunlight. He blinks his eyes, throws his head back and lowers the blind. But as soon as he releases it, the blind springs back up. He tries a couple of times, then, at the third attempt, holds it down with his hand. Behind him a family is unwrapping eatables (a dry sausage, cheese, etc.).

At the back of the bus, the hysterical woman looks strained. She is dripping with sweat and mops herself mechanically with her handkerchief.

Shot, in the foreground, of the fan rhythmically fanning the old lady's face.

Engine noise.

Shot, in the foreground, of the handkerchief rhythmically mopping the face of the woman at the back.

Shot of the fan.

Two men's faces as they sleep, openmouthed. Their necks protruding from open shirts, their heads swaying.

Shot of the fan.

The bus roof. The Malay is in pain. He gets to his knees and scratches himself. He falls back into a sitting position. He tries to shade himself by balancing one of the parcels between the trunk and the pram. He scratches himself.

Shot of bus roof from above. The bus moves away in the desert.

Overwhelming impression of loneliness and heat.

Inside the bus. Nellie and Tom, face to camera. Tom is dozing. A hard-faced Nellie is looking straight ahead.

He groans.

NELLIE (*her voice is weary and almost muffled, but it is still harsh*): Give me a cigarette.

TOM: Eh? Oh, yes . . .

Tom is startled.

He fumbles in his pockets and hands her his packet. She takes a cigarette and lights it.

On Nellie. She is smoking with a sort of drab sensuality, not blowing the smoke from her mouth, but letting her lower jaw drop a little and leaving the smoke to rise from her open mouth.

On the two of them.

NELLIE: When does it leave?

TOM: What?

NELLIE: The *São Paolo*. When does it leave?

TOM: The day after tomorrow . . .

Nellie's face lights up and she sighs with relief.

NELLIE: The day after tomorrow . . .

Tom gives her a black look.

TOM: You're in a hurry to get home, eh? Can't wait?

NELLIE: If you knew how sick I was of . . .

TOM (*ironic*): Sick of what?

NELLIE: Of everything. Of the sun for starters. I could happily go 10 years without seeing the sun again. And then all the creatures that go with it— the bugs, the spiders, the scorpions, the tarantulas. And the pigsties you have to sing in. And the men in those pigsties. And their eyes roving all over your body. And their hands. I could almost bless the typhus. But for that, we'd have been another month in Santareya.

Tom sniggers.

TOM: And me?

NELLIE: What about you?

TOM: You're not sick of me, are you?

Nellie shrugs her shoulders.

NELLIE: Oh yes, Tom! You make me sick, you know. Deeply sick. But not

Silence. She goes on smoking, hard-faced. He falls back into drowsiness.

View of the desert. The road begins to climb. There are rocks visible on the horizon. The bus travels along the road, its windows glinting in the sun.

The roof of the bus. The Malay (medium shot). He seems in terrible pain. He is scratching himself and writhing convulsively. He tries to get to his knees, then falls flat on his stomach, head first, so that his head is protruding beyond the roof above the bonnet of the vehicle.

The back of the driver's head, with the windscreen visible beyond him. The wipers are still. Through the glass we see the road. It has become a narrow, winding coast road now. Suddenly, the landscape is hidden by a dark, sticky stream of liquid. It is running down on to the windscreen from outside. The driver switches on the wipers.

Close-up of the wipers swishing over the blood.

as much as I do myself. But what's to be done? I'm stuck with you.

NELLIE'S VOICE (*quieter, almost whispering*): I'm sick of it, Tom. I'm sick of the sun.

The driver's face, shot directly from the front, his eyes wide with horror. The driver's foot pressed hard down on the accelerator.

Shot of Tom and the driver face to camera.

TOM: What's wrong?

DRIVER: What's wrong is that your lady friend's really gone and done it!'

TOM: What has she done?

DRIVER: She's got us carrying a typhus victim, that's what.

Shot of the interior from the back of the bus. Some are standing, others leaning forward. They are shouting.

VARIOUS VOICES: What's wrong? What's wrong? What's happening?

The driver turns round to them, continuing to accelerate.

DRIVER: Well, we're in a fine old mess. The brother up there has just spewed blood all over the windscreen!

External shot of the bus, as it rushes along the twisty road, taking the bends on two wheels. The Malay's head sticks out beyond the roof.

Inside the bus. A rapid succession of faces in close-up.

The face of the old lady, the wife of the noble old gentleman.

OLD LADY: You're a criminal, young lady. A criminal!

The face of the hysterical woman.

THE WOMAN: Faster! Faster! Put your foot down. Let's get away!

The face of the old lady with the fan. Her smile has disappeared. She seems panicky and is fanning herself faster and faster.

Face of the 10-year-old boy.

BOY: Mummy, what's going to happen to us? What's going to happen to us?

Interior of the bus, seen from the right. People standing and leaning forward.

SOME: Put your foot down! Quicker!

OTHERS: Stop! Stop!

The old gentleman has stood up.

OLD GENTLEMAN: You're mad, driver. Stop this minute. We can't go on with that above our heads.

Tom has leaned over the driver.

TOM: Do you hear what they're saying? Are you going to stop for Christ's sake! We've got to throw the man off, I tell you.

NELLIE: And what if he's still alive?

On Nellie.

Nellie, Tom, the driver—from the side. Tom rounds angrily on Nellie.

TOM: Oh no, you're not going to be a pain in the neck again?! You got us into this mess. Right now, let me try and get us out of it.

The driver, full-length. He depresses the clutch and brakes. Gear change. Hand brake.

Shot of the bus from the outside. It slides to a halt. Tom and the driver get out. The driver gives Tom a leg up. He climbs on to the roof and helps the driver climb up behind him. Tom leans over the Malay.

DRIVER: Is he still alive?

TOM: I don't know. Give me a hand.

Tom is quaking with fear and anger. They slide the Malay's body to the edge of the roof, his legs dangling over the side. Tom jumps down on to the road. The driver, who has stayed on the roof, takes the Malay by the shoulders and lowers him. Tom takes him in his arms but lets go immediately, recoiling in horror. The driver gets down from the roof. The Malay is stretched out on the road, eyes blank, mouth open and fists clenched. Tom and the driver stand in front of the lifeless body, looking on with revulsion. Tom wipes his brow with his handkerchief.

DRIVER: Hey, he's still warm!

TOM: Oh, never mind that. It's him or us, isn't it? Tell them he was dead. It's likely that he is.

The driver and Tom get back on the bus.

The interior of the bus, shot from the front. The three seats belonging to Nellie, Tom and the driver. The driver and Tom pass Nellie on the way back to their places. The driver puts the bus into first gear. Nellie gives Tom a hard stare. Tom says nothing.

The people in the bus (seen face to camera) are silent and tense.

Tom and Nellie shot face-on. Tom looks at Nellie hesitantly. Nellie looks straight ahead.

He was dead, Nellie.

NELLIE: Are you sure? Are you sure he was?

TOM: Already cold.

On Tom.

The road. The body in close-up. In the distance, the bus recedes into the distance and disappears round a bend. The camera pulls back to show the abandoned body out in the rocky desert.

*

*

A quayside at the end of a dry dock. In the background, a ship with workers repainting its hull. The quayside is deserted and grass is growing between the cobblestones. There are kids playing 'prisoner's base' on the left. George appears. He is staggering along at the quay's edge. He is drunk. A bottle of whisky in his left-hand pocket. He stumbles and almost falls into the water. He tries to get up and just manages to sit himself down on the edge of the quay, his legs dangling over the water.

George, full-length, sitting on the edge of the quay (shot face to camera—in fact from the water and from below). He has a pasty look about him. He laughs.

GEORGE (*laughing*): That would have been no great loss. Oh, no. No great loss

He pulls the bottle from his pocket and drinks straight from it. He wags his finger in a gesture of ironic denial.

No. No great loss.

He leans over and looks at the water, apparently fascinated. It seems as though he is going to let himself slip. Then he gathers himself again. His face is hard, hate-filled and tight-lipped.

That would be too easy.

He takes the bottle, puts the cork in and throws it into the water.

Shot of the bottle floating.

Full-length shot of the kids, huddled together. They are looking in George's direction.

ONE OF THE KIDS: It's George! Watch this.

The kid picks up a pebble and throws it.

George from behind. The pebble hits him between the shoulder blades. He turns round.

Shot of George and the kids. The kids burst out laughing.

THE KIDS: Drunkard! Drunkard!

George tries with difficulty to stand up.

GEORGE: Come here, you little vermin! Filthy little Whites!

The kids draw back, a little anxious. George gets to his knees and falls on his back on the quayside. Feeling safer, the kids move towards him, shouting.

THE KIDS: Drunkard! Drunkard!

George in the foreground, seen from above. Head and shoulders. He has a broad smile and glassy eyes.

Shot of the bottle aimlessly drifting away.

GEORGE (*stammering*): Go ahead! Take the mickey! I enjoy it.

*

*

In the bus. Silence. The people watching each other out of the corner of their eyes.

Nellie and Tom. Tom has an absorbed, worried expression. Nellie looks at Tom, then looks straight ahead. Tom has a strange air about him. It is as though he is studying something deep inside him. Nellie looks at him again. On Nellie: she seems both horrified and fascinated. On Tom (from waist up): he slowly raises his right hand, which is a little tense, plunges it into his shirt at chest level and begins scratching himself. Nellie's face is a terrifying picture of fear and loathing. Tom's hands scratching (foreground). Then Tom's head and shoulders. His contorted expression of tense pleasure and rage, while his hands go on scratching away beneath his shirt.

*

The quayside. George, shot full-length, gets up with difficulty. The quayside is deserted. He starts off. Seen from behind, he staggers and limps along.

George outside the town, seen from behind on the road. On the right a mud-built house, on the left a patch of waste ground. The road stretches ahead as far as the eye can see. He passes the mud house, goes off the road and on to the waste ground. In the distance before him, there are native huts or cabins, difficult to make out.

George, still shot from behind, has reached the huts we saw in the distance. He is in a shanty town. Wretched native huts made from the casings of petrol cans. We see four or five huts: two on the right, one on the left, one or two further off. He slips in between the huts and the camera follows him. He comes up to one of the huts that was originally further off and calls out.

GEORGE: Sakki!

The old curtain hanging at the entrance to the hut is pulled back. A native appears and comes out, stooping to get under the door.

George and Sakki shot from the side.

SAKKI: What do you want?

GEORGE: Stash the rice somewhere and clear out. You're going to get a visit from the cops.

SAKKI: Who told you that?

The Malay regards him with distrust. George hiccups.

GEORGE: I just know. Best to scarper, I tell you.

SAKKI: You're drunk.

GEORGE: Never mind that. I'm drunk, but you can trust me. Get out of here.

The Malay goes back into his hut muttering.

George, full-length and from behind, outside the hut. He shrugs his shoulders and walks on.

George from behind. He is walking through a sort of scrubland (bare heath-land with a few bushes). In the distance, a lonely, wretched cabin.

George outside the cabin. Evening is falling. A dog runs out to him yelping, wagging its tail. George, still from behind, gives it a kick.

In your kennel, drunkard's mutt!

He pushes open the door.

Interior of the cabin: a table, a rush mat on the floor, an old rocking chair, a barrel full of water. Against the wall, above the table, a photograph of George in a white uniform.

George full-length, in profile. He goes towards the table and looks up at the photograph. He gazes at it expression-less, but at some length.

The cabin seen from the door. George turns away from the photograph, goes over to the rush mat and falls on it. He writhes about a little, then begins to snore.

Shot of the bottle floating on the water (the waves are a little stronger).

*

*

A large square on the outskirts of Ottawee. A circular, bare patch of ground. The road runs alongside the patch of land. On the other side of the roadway, a pavement lined with build-ings. The camera takes in only one third of the square: a portion of the patch of bare earth, a segment of road and a few buildings beside the pavement. These are a petrol station, a little white building in reinforced concrete with two pumps beside the pavement, a big white block of flats of seven or eight storeys, with a cafe—Terminus Café—on the ground floor and, in front of it, a post with a sign reading SPRING COACHES, OTTAWEE–SANTAREYA, TERMINUS. On the other side of the cafe is a patch of waste ground, then three or four wretched little shacks. The whole has the air of an area on the outskirts of the town where a number of European buildings have sprung up like mushrooms. Further on, directly ahead of the camera, to the right of the cafe and the shacks, a large, dark, sinister, four-storey building with about 30 barred windows and a heavy, dark door. Above the door: CHAVOZ HOSPITAL.

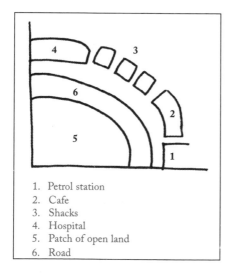

1. Petrol station
2. Cafe
3. Shacks
4. Hospital
5. Patch of open land
6. Road

Outside the cafe, 20 or so people standing around waiting. Some are pacing up and down, others standing still near the post with the sign, facing the camera, as though scanning the horizon. The camera moves towards them.

Shot of seven or eight people standing waiting, with the signpost in the centre and the cafe behind them. Silence. Fixed stares.

A man starts, as though waking.

A middle-aged lady on the verge of tears.

Silence. The man begins to pace up and down.

A clock strikes seven.

MAN: Seven o'clock. It's an hour and a half late.

LADY: I'm horribly worried—my two sons are on it.[1]

If only we could get through on the phone, we'd know if they've set off.

A YOUNG WOMAN: Well, can't we?

LADY: We can't. Santareya's not answering.

Silence. Heads and shoulders of the people waiting. Suddenly, the faces light up. They have seen the bus.

MANY VOICES: There it is! There it is!

The square, seen as before.

The bus. People are already pressing to the edge of the pavement. Some are even in the roadway, waving.

Prolonged, searing blast on a horn, like a siren.

But the bus sweeps by, hooting its horn. People are only just able to jump back on to the pavement. Then, after a second's hesitation, and as though by some unspoken accord, they run after the bus which slows and comes to a halt outside the hospital.

The bus seen from the front, against the kerb. The pavement and the hospital facade. In the background, the people running up. The driver gets out of the bus and turns to them.

DRIVER: Get back! Get back! Typhus!

The people step back, not knowing what to do. The hospital door opens and nurses come out.

A NURSE: Do you have any sick passengers?

DRIVER: Definitely one. I don't know about the others.

The two twins get off the bus. The lady, whom we see face to camera, tries to rush towards them. The twins seem unsure what to do. They turn towards their mother, but do not answer. A male nurse prevents the lady from coming through.

LADY: Martha! Lucy!

But they're my daughters. I want . . .

MALE NURSE: We're going to ask you to be a bit patient, madam. You'll be able to find out how they are every day, but we're going to have to isolate them for a while.

The bearded man and the man with the moustache get off the bus.

Bearded man, in a woeful tone:

MAN IN THE CROWD: Hello, Fred.

BEARDED MAN: Hello, Timmy.

TIMMY: You're not the one who's ill, are you?

BEARDED MAN (*even more woefully*): I don't know, Tim, I don't know. It could be me.

The old gentleman and lady and other passengers get off the bus. People in the crowd wave and call to them, but they barely respond, walking off stiffly and mechanically. The nurses take them into the hospital. Nellie and Tom get off. Tom is leaning on Nellie and seems in pain. He is carrying the birdcage. Leaning on Nellie, he moves off with her.

The crowd suddenly falls silent.

Head and shoulders of the people in the crowd. We do not see Tom, but we can see that they are staring after him and the camera moves along the line of faces of the crowd, as if they are being seen through the eyes of Tom and Nellie.

A nurse rushes up and supports Tom. A nurse to Nellie:

NURSE: This way, madam. Women this way.

Nellie and Tom shot full-length outside the hospital door. A female nurse by Nellie and a male nurse holding Tom up. They stop and turn to each other.

NELLIE: Goodbye, Tom.

TOM (*nastily*): You're a lucky devil. There's nothing wrong with you.

Tom moves off again with difficulty and goes into the hospital. Before entering, Nellie turns round and casts a long look behind her. Then she looks up at the sky, as in a farewell gesture. Then she takes the nurse's arm and goes in herself.

Dissolve.

The quayside. The *São Paulo* is leaving for Europe. They take the gangplank away. A crowd on the quayside. On the deck, passengers wave their handkerchiefs.

Sirens.

*   *

A hospital ward. Bare walls. From left to right: a window looking out to sea and three beds along the wall. The first of these is empty and unmade, the second has not been slept in. An old woman is sleeping in the third. A nurse, shot full-length, is sitting in a wicker chair at the foot of the first bed. Nellie is by the window, her back to the camera, her face pressed against the pane. Through the window, we can see the *São Paulo* sailing away. Nellie turns around. She seems weary. She is dressed shabbily in a pinafore top and grey skirt, the patient's uniform.

NELLIE: That's it. It's gone.

NURSE: You'll be on the next one. There's nothing wrong with you. That's definite now.

NELLIE: When will I be able to leave?

NURSE: You'll have to be patient for four more days.

Nellie goes back to the bed and sits on it.

NELLIE: There are times I think I'll never see Europe again.

NURSE: Come on, don't be silly! What sort of talk is that. You've got to get a grip. I bet you'll be home in three months.

NELLIE: I would so like that. I still have a chance in Europe. But not here (*she shudders*). It must be horrible to die here.

NURSE: Don't even think about it! Tell me what you're going to do back home. Sing?

NELLIE: No, not sing. I've done too much singing. I'm going to work. I'd like to start over again.

A silence. Her face first expresses a sort of hope, then darkens. She looks weary and resigned once more.

And Tom? Tom Skeener? How is he today? Will I be able to see him soon?

NURSE (*softly*): I don't think so. I don't think you'll be able to see him again.

*

*

Tom in a hospital bed. His body wasted and his eyes feverish. The bird cage hangs above his bed. A male nurse is standing beside it.

Chirpings of the bird.

The nurse doesn't reply.

TOM: So, I'm done for, am I?

47

The nurse gets up, unhooks the cage and puts it on the bed. Tom opens the cage, puts his arm in and grabs the bird. He withdraws his arm from the cage, still holding the bird tight in his fist. The cage falls on to the floor.

Tom opens his hand. The dead bird falls on to the white sheet.

Tom sniggers.

OK. I get it. Pass me the cage.

Frantic chirping, then silence.

MALE NURSE: What are you doing?

TOM: There's what I'm doing.

NURSE: You brute!

TOM: This way, I won't die alone.

A silence. Tom has picked up the bird and is looking at it.

TOM (*still staring at the bird*): How's Nellie Dixmier?

NURSE: She's not infected.

TOM: The cow!

NURSE: Do you want me to give her a message?

TOM: No.

NURSE: Are . . . are you leaving her anything?

TOM: That would hurt. She's going to survive. You don't want me to help her as well, do you?

He holds out the bird to him.

The nurse hesitates. Then he takes the bird, goes to an open window and throws it out.

The nurse exits. Shot of Tom alone, lying still, his eyes wide open.

Shot of the *São Paulo* moving off towards the open sea.

Sling it out of the window.

Right now, go. I'm going to wait.

*

*

A room in the hospital. Behind a long counter, nurses are putting infected objects belonging to the patients into piles. Two or three clerks at tables.

The shot: the counter which reaches out beyond the screen to right and left, the tables and the clerks. Behind these, the nurses coming and going. The bearded man at the counter is sorting his things into his cases.

CLERK: Is it all there?

BEARDED MAN: Yes.

CLERK: Will you sign here?'

The bearded man signs a register. The old gentleman and lady come in.

They come up to the counter.

OLD GENTLEMAN: Is this where we get our things back?

CLERK: Yes, sir. We've disinfected and sterilized them. What number?

OLD GENTLEMAN: 92 and 57.

CLERK (*to a female nurse*): The things for 92 and 57. (*To the old gentleman*) Well, all in all, you've got off lightly there.

OLD GENTLEMAN: But what foolhardiness, sir, what terrible foolhardiness! The whole city could be contaminated.

CLERK (*smiling*): So it could. But there's no fear of that now. We've nipped it in the bud. Just sign here, please.

They bring the couple's effects.

A clerk comes in with Tom's things and his empty birdcage. He puts everything down on the counter near the second table.

Here are number 29's effects.

Nellie comes in. She approaches the old lady and gentleman.

On the old lady. She looks Nellie up and down with a lorgnette and leaves, followed by the old gentleman, without a word to her.

Nellie goes over to the counter.

NELLIE: Number 32, please.

Shot of the empty cage on the counter in the foreground.

Nellie, full-length from behind. She turns to the cage. She touches it slowly, running her hand along the bars, as though caressing it. A pause.

(*Shot from behind—to the clerk*): Is he dead?

CLERK: Number 29? This morning at five o'clock.

Nellie from behind, from the waist up. Silent. Only her shoulders, twitching convulsively, betray her state of mind.

NELLIE: Did he leave a message for me?

CLERK: I don't think so.

NELLIE: And he's left me nothing?

CLERK: No, miss. Nothing. Will you check nothing is missing?

Nellie's things are placed on the table.

NELLIE (*in a gentle, strangled voice*): No, no. It's all fine.

CLERK: Then, will you sign here?

Nellie signs. She puts her things into a case with a wavering hand.

NELLIE: Can I take the cage?

CLERK: Oh, the cage. Yes, if you want.

Nellie turns around and makes to leave. She is carrying a large case and the cage. She has a soft face, but harrowed and ravaged. The camera approaches her, showing her head and shoulders first, then a close-up of her face.

The street outside the hospital. Nellie full-length, face to camera. She has put the cage and the case down on the pavement. She rummages in her bag and pulls out two banknotes and some coins. Despair in her face. Passers-by coming and going behind her. An ambulance car rushes by, blowing its horn. Nellie only just has time to jump back on the pavement before she is run over.

The motor ambulance. It has stopped a few yards further on. We see it from the back. Its back doors open and two stretcher-bearers get out carrying a native on a stretcher. The camera follows them, as they go into the hospital.

Shot of the hospital entrance hall. An enormous concourse with a double staircase at the end of it. A nurse, sitting at a table, with the register of patients.

The stretcher-bearers approach her and put the stretcher down on the slab floor.

The nurse and a stretcher-bearer standing at the table. The nurse dips a pen in an inkwell.

NURSE: Where's he from?

STRETCHER-BEARER: Shantytown.

NURSE: What's wrong with him?

STRETCHER-BEARER: Don't know. They think it's typhus.

On the nurse (head and shoulders). Her face has grown serious. She writes.

The nurse (from behind) and the register. We see her writing in a large, careful hand: 'Typhus?'

On the pavement, Nellie, shot full-length, rummages in her bag. She is holding the coins and notes in her left hand. With the right, she pulls a coin out of her bag. Visibly, this is all she has left. She puts all of it back in the bag, seems to make up her mind and goes back into the hospital.

The director's office. A large desk. A stout, white-haired man behind the desk, with a handsome, hard, if somewhat bloated, face. Nellie at the desk, shot from behind. She is explaining nervously.

NELLIE: We were paid before we left Santareya. We were expecting to leave for Europe. He had all our money.

DIRECTOR: Do you have any documents to prove this?

On Nellie, in profile.
On the director, face to camera.

NELLIE: I have nothing.

DIRECTOR: This is obviously very awkward. But we're forced to hold the money until we have further information.

Still on the director.

NELLIE'S VOICE (*quiet, ashamed*): I haven't a penny to my name.

DIRECTOR: You weren't . . . you weren't his wife?

On Nellie, head and shoulders, face to camera.

NELLIE: No.

A pause.

NELLIE: I . . . I was . . .

Nellie and the director, in profile.

DIRECTOR: I understand. But I'm sorry, there's nothing we can do.

He gets up to see her out. We see Nellie and the director, face to camera, walking to the door. The director stops.

(*Hesitating*): I could advance you something from my personal fund . . .

NELLIE (*as if afraid*): No, no . . . Thank you, sir. I'll try and sort something out.

There's a knock at the door.

DIRECTOR: Come in.

The door. It opens. Thomas, a young hospital doctor, comes in.

Nellie appears by the door.

DR THOMAS: Am I disturbing you?

NELLIE (*in a soft voice, as though humiliated*): No, I was going. Goodbye, gentlemen.

She leaves.

Thomas and the director standing in the middle of the office, full-length. The director shot face to camera, Thomas shot in three-quarter view.

DR THOMAS: They've just brought a native in . . .

DIRECTOR: Yes?

DR THOMAS: It's a typhus case.

The director throws his arms wide and lowers his head.

DIRECTOR: Oh, no!

*

*

The bottle tossed by the waves.

George on the quayside with his dog. He is walking slowly, but not staggering. He is holding a ball of rags.

George, side view, stooping. He shows the dog the ball and throws it into the distance.

GEORGE: Go on, fetch, drunkard's mutt! Go and fetch it right now!

The dog runs and brings back the ball. As it is coming back towards George, a funeral procession comes out of a neighbouring street. Shot of George in the foreground, with the dog running towards him on the quayside. Behind them, facing the audience, the street the funeral procession is coming out of. It turns and goes along the quayside. It is a pauper's funeral. The cheapest type of hearse. Behind it, Nellie alone; far behind Nellie, a representative of the hospital, a little fat man looking cheerful and unconcerned.

The hearse passes by George. George, full-length and in profile, in the foreground. He hesitates, casts a hard look at Nellie, then looks at the ball he has taken from the dog's mouth. Then, suddenly, he makes up his mind. He shows the dog the ball.

Fetch! Fetch it quick!

He throws it towards the funeral. The dog bounds off.

Shot of Nellie, full-length, behind the hearse. The dog picks up the ball almost between her legs. She nearly falls. She gathers herself and levels a contemptuous stare at George.

George in the foreground, his head turned three-quarters away from us, towards Nellie. He watches her. Nellie walks slowly and carries on watching him. The dog runs from Nellie to George with the ball in its mouth. The dog comes up to George who pays it no attention and continues to watch Nellie. The dog presses against its owner and rubs its head against his trousers to get his attention. George takes the ball from the dog's mouth, stands up straight again and watches Nellie go by (he is now being shot from behind; we see his head turn in the direction the funeral is taking) and puts the ball back in his pocket.

Dissolve.

The cemetery gate. We can just make out gravestones through the gate. Nellie comes out. She is walking with the same lazy, slouching gait as George before. She walks on, looking gloomy and vacant.

George in a busy street. Slouching gait, and a gloomy, vacant air.

Nellie in a European-type main street. She is moving lethargically, bumping into people as she walks, not paying attention. Several turn round and look at her.

George. He stops in front of a cafe and looks at it.

Nellie. She stops in front of a large poster, which reads: '"The Mount Everest". Nightclub—Floorshow— Open All Night.' She takes a long look at it, then turns round and approaches a policeman on the edge of the pavement. Evening is falling and the lights are coming on.

NELLIE: Can you tell me how to get to the 'Mount Everest'?

*

*

The nightclub. The camera moves between the tables through a smoky atmosphere. This is the area reserved for natives. Some are drinking, sitting at rough tables; others are sitting on the floor, playing cards or dice. Only men are present. The camera moves across the room and comes up to a large wooden partition, about four feet high, separating the native cafe area from the European bar. Passage between the two is through a gate on the left. The camera passes through the partition. On the European side, there is a bar on the left, little tables or barrels and wicker chairs around the tables. At the back, a little stage with its curtain down. There is a fairly pathetic band of two guitarists and an upright piano. The pianist is sitting on his stool facing the audience. He is drinking a beer. The guitarists are playing absent-mindedly, talking together and laughing.

There are few clients on the European side. Men only. Two fair-haired sailors, very stiff, drinking whisky at the same table without exchanging a word. Further on, near the door, a little man

Conversations and noises of all kinds, more or less drowning out a shrill, monotonous tune on the guitar.

The sound of conversation fades until it merely provides a background, as it were, to the guitar music.

with a goatee beard and a bowler hat. In the centre, Nogaro, tall and flabby, with a spineless, cruel look about him, is sitting at a table playing patience. The owner, Mercutio, a short, lame man, almost bald, is walking between the tables. He comes over to Nogaro.

Nogaro and the owner coming over to him. In the background, a tall white woman appears. She is ugly, quite old and bare-thighed.

THE WOMAN (*in a languid, cracked voice*): And now, Miss Padmavati, favourite dancer of the King of Cambodia!

The curtain rises, the piano plays, a native comes on and begins to dance. This is all in the background. In the foreground we see Nogaro and the owner, standing at his table. Nogaro turns around languidly, leaving a hand holding a card in the air.

The owner shrugs his shoulders.

NOGARO: Another Malay!

OWNER: I take what I can find.

Nogaro points round at the customers with the hand that is holding the card.

NOGARO: Yes, and look at your customers! Do you think they want to see Malays?

The two sailors are drinking in silence, their back turned to the Malay girl. The little man in the bowler hat is smiling pensively, his eyes fixed on the cocktail bar.

On Nogaro.

Don't you see, they're sick of Malays. They see them all day long. And they smell of fish glue. Not everyone likes fish glue.

He puts the card on the table and turns up two others.

(*Looking down at his game of patience*): You used to have pretty little blonde dolls. That's what brought the crowds in.

Nogaro and the owner.

OWNER: Where do you think I'm going to find them? Everyone's clearing out on account of the typhus. The stripper at the 'Alcazar' left last week on the *São Paulo*.

Pause. Nogaro looks at the Malay girl.

NOGARO: She is *so* ugly!

The owner shrugs his shoulders.

OWNER: How is it with the typhus now?

NOGARO: Dunno. There was one case at the hospital, but I haven't heard of any others. I think it's under control.

OWNER: It'd better be. It'd better stop. Otherwise, I'm closing down.

Nogaro smiles.

He leans over his game of patience and turns up some cards.

NOGARO: Oh, you know. Even where there's typhus, there's still money to be made.

*   *

Night. Nellie in a deserted alley, dimly
lit by an oil lamp. She is in a hurry. A
man is there, a motionless, indistinct
shape in the darkness. She bumps into
him. It's George. He looks at her and
smiles. She cries out softly. George
holds out his hand.

GEORGE: What is it? No need to be
afraid of me. I'm harmless.

Nellie screams, pushes him away and
runs off. He watches her, sniggering,
and goes on his way.

The night club. Area reserved for the
natives (shot from the European bar).
At the back of this area, there is a door.
Nellie appears in the doorway right at
the back. She hesitates, then takes a few
steps forward. The natives turn to look
at her. She comes forward a little more.
Some natives stand up and move
towards her. She stops.

The owner and Nogaro shot face to
camera, turned towards the back of the
club.

OWNER: What is that?

NOGARO: It's a little mouse that's come
in through the wrong door.

The owner gestures to an athletic, half-naked Malay, who comes over to him.

OWNER (*to the Malay*): Go fetch her, Rikko.

The partition in the foreground. In the background, Nellie and the natives. She pushes them away. At the side, the Malay pushes open the little gate, passes through the partition, moves the Malays aside and brings Nellie back.

Nellie, the owner and Nogaro, shot full-length. Nogaro is shuffling the cards.

Nogaro raises his head.

What can I do for you?

NELLIE: I'm a singer.

NOGARO (*flirtatiously*): You can sing for me any time.

NELLIE (*pretending not to understand*): That is what I do.

OWNER: And?

NELLIE: I was thinking you might like to hire me to sing.

OWNER: Where you from?

Nellie is taken aback by his directness, but gets a grip on herself.

NELLIE: Santareya. I was singing at the 'Eldorado'. I left on account of the typhus.

OWNER: Can you dance? The artistes dance with the customers here when they've finished their sets. You get the basic rate plus three per cent on the bottles you sell.

NELLIE: That's not the kind of work I'm really fond of.

OWNER: Take it or leave it.

NELLIE: I'll take it.

Nellie shrugs her shoulders.

Nogaro has been looking at her for a while. Undressing her with his eyes. Nellie becomes uncomfortable and turns her head away. Nogaro carries on looking at her, gently licking his lips.

OWNER: We'll give her a run-out this evening.

NOGARO: A run-out. And, as there won't be many people here this evening, she can save the dance after her act for me. Can't you, doll?

Nellie nods. The owner calls the Malay servant.

OWNER: Take the young lady to dressing room three. (*To Nellie*) I'm ready and waiting.

Nellie cursorily nods assent and exits. Nogaro stares after her, then lays out the cards for his game of patience.

NOGARO (*to Owner*): Lucky blighter!

OWNER: Bah.

NOGARO: Come off it, you have all the luck. She's gonna make you a fortune.

OWNER: She isn't in the first flush of youth.

NOGARO: No, but she's well stacked. You only had to watch the sailors there when she was talking. Bet you they don't turn their backs on her like they do on your Malays.

OWNER: I wonder if she has much of a voice?

NOGARO: Oh, the voice . . .

Nogaro makes a broad gesture indicating indifference.

The entrance door to the native bar area. George comes in and the camera pulls back. George wanders between the tables. He stops by a Malay who is seated on the ground and playing cards.

GEORGE: Can you buy me a drink?

THE MALAY: I'm cleaned out. (*Pointing to another player*) He's won the lot.

George sets off again, hesitantly (shot full-length, in profile). He goes as far as the partition and leans his elbows on it, his eyes staring off into space.

Nogaro, alone at his table. He is playing patience. The owner at the back of the club is talking to a Malay servant. Nellie appears. She comes forward hesitantly. Nogaro looks up and sees her.

Nellie stops.

Nellie comes over to him.

Without getting up, Nogaro takes her by the arm and forces her to sit down.

The owner turns round.

Nellie, stiff and embarrassed, laughs nervously.

NOGARO: Hey, doll!

Come and sit down.

Oh, you don't wanna sit down? It's because we haven't been introduced? Well, there we are, I'm Nogaro. What's your name?

NELLIE: Nellie Dixmier.

NOGARO: Now, now, I'm gonna give you a bit of advice, doll. You should always be *very* nice to me, because I'm the owner's best friend. Isn't that right, Mercutio? Hey, Mercutio!

OWNER: What?

NOGARO: Isn't it right that I'm your best friend?

MERCUTIO: Up yours!

NOGARO: You see! You wouldn't believe how fond he is of me.

Everybody's fond of me. I'm like a drug. They just can't get enough of me.

On Nellie. She is laughing. She has turned her head away a little and, to retain her composure, is looking over to the native bar. Suddenly, her face stiffens and she strangles back a scream.

Nellie recovers her composure and replies reluctantly.

What's the matter, babe?

NELLIE: It's nothing.

NOGARO: Seen a face here you don't like the look of?

NELLIE: It's that chap over there, leaning on the partition. He gave me a fright just now in the street. There, there, that Malay.

Nogaro and Nellie seen from the European bar. Nogaro has turned round. In the background, George, with a cigarette in his mouth, who seems in a dream, paying them no attention. Nogaro begins to laugh.

Nellie's eyes remain riveted on George.

NOGARO: Who? George? But he isn't a Malay. Yes, he dresses like that, but it's just for effect. You shouldn't be afraid of George, now! He's a nice guy. He's a little bitter, 'cos he's seen some bad times, but he's all right deep down. And he has a great little party trick. He often entertains us with it. You'll see.

Nogaro takes his riding whip from the table and stands up. Nellie looks worried.

NELLIE: What are you going to do?

NOGARO: Have you seen the bear dance?

NELLIE: Leave him, please. I . . . I don't like to look at him.

Nogaro goes over to George, not listening to her.

Nogaro on one side of the partition, George on the other.

Shot from the waist up. George hasn't seen him coming. He has a distant look in his eye.

NOGARO: Evening, George.

George is startled. He looks at him.

GEORGE: Evening.

NOGARO: Not getting much whisky, eh?

George groans but doesn't reply.

Nogaro lifts George's chin with the tip of his riding whip.

NOGARO: Will you look at me when I'm talking to you? Can't you be nice? I like people to be nice to me.

GEORGE: What do you want?

NOGARO: I want to buy you a bottle of whisky. But you're going to be a poppet and do the bear dance for us first.

GEORGE: I won't.

NOGARO: Oh, Georgie, you won't? So you've gone off whisky?

GEORGE: I won't.

Nogaro taps him very gently, almost caressingly, on the cheeks with his whip.

The two of them in the foreground. Head and shoulders. Nogaro is looking at George and grabs him by the shoulder.

The two shot full-length. Behind them we see natives casually coming closer, slyly interested. Nogaro, still holding George by the shoulder, leads him through the gate. George, his head lowered, downcast and unresisting, allows himself to be led. Nogaro and George move towards the middle of the European bar. The camera retreats as they advance. More and more curious, amused bystanders gradually press themselves to the wooden partition behind them.

NOGARO: George, that makes me very unhappy. You're not being nice. Not nice at all. I can't stand people who aren't nice. That really gets my goat. You see, you're going to make a very big mistake. You're going to get me mad, and who knows what I might do then. Afterwards, I'll be sorry, of course. And so will you. But the harm will have been done by then. Come on George, be a good boy. You don't want me to get angry, do you? You're going to be nice to me? Eh? Eh?

GEORGE (*grunting quietly*): Filthy Whites! Bastards!

69

Nogaro raises his whip.

NOGARO: What's that you said, George?

GEORGE: All right. I'll dance.

Without letting go of George's shoulder, Nogaro turns round to the whole company.

NOGARO: Sparing no expense, the manager of the 'Mount Everest' club commands me to introduce an exceptional, nay sensational, attraction: the Bear Dance! Take your seats, ladies and gentlemen, the show is about to begin!

George looks wretched and distraught.

Shot of laughing Malays with cigars in their mouths leaning on the low railing.

Shot of the native bar opposite, the door at the back. Malays are getting up and rushing to join their friends. We see them from behind now, jammed together.

George brings his elbows back to his chest and sticks out his forearms, letting his hands hang limp to represent the forepaws of a bear standing on its hind legs. Nogaro cracks his whip.

Full-length shot of Nellie. She has stood up and is gripping the back of a chair with her hand, looking on horrified at the scene.

George begins to waddle heavily, like a bear. The waddling is very slow at first.

Shot of the sailors, laughing for all they are worth.

George's face in the foreground, his eyes almost white, his mouth contorted. He looks in pain.

George and Nogaro. Nogaro cracks his whip in the air.

Faster! Faster!

George begins to dance faster. George's face in a close-up, bobbing around as he dances.

Shot of Nellie. The owner passes by, laughing, with a cigar in his mouth. She puts her hand on his arm. He gives her a sardonic smile.

NELLIE: Stop them!

They've no right to humiliate a man like that.

OWNER: Humiliate who? George? If you think they can humiliate him any more! . . . He's a wreck of a man.

Nogaro and George in the middle of the room. The Malays behind the barrier.

NOGARO: Faster! Faster!

Nogaro is slashing at the ground with his whip and George is forced to jump to avoid being hit. The dance quickens. The Malays clap in time with his dancing.

MALAYS: Hi! Hi! Hi! . . .

George shot full-length, face to camera, in the background. In the foreground, Nellie shot head and shoulders, seen from behind. George suddenly notices Nellie and stops dead. He looks at her.

George and Nogaro full-length, face to camera. Nogaro strikes out with his whip at George's feet but George does not try to avoid the blow. He does not even seem to feel it. He looks at Nellie.

Nellie and George full-length, in profile. Nogaro, dumbfounded, a little way behind George. George and Nellie look at each other. George takes a few steps towards Nellie, who remains motionless and maintains her hard stare.

A silence.

GEORGE (*in a wheezy voice*): You were here! You saw me dance! Well, what do you think of it? I'm a joker, eh? One helluva joker?!

Nellie makes no reply. George, seen from behind, full-length. Nellie, facing the camera beyond him. She keeps up her hard stare.

Since you like entertainment, I'll tell you a little story. It won't cost you anything, I'll throw it in for free. You

George, head and shoulders, face to camera. He can barely speak.

George, full-length, face to camera. Nogaro alongside him.

Nogaro raises his whip and hits George on the head with the pommel. George falls.

George on the ground, face to camera, the upper part of his body raised, supporting himself on the palms of his hands, his eyes flashing with anger. Nogaro leaning over him with his riding whip raised. George tries to get up, but falls back down.

know what the galleys were? Floating prisons. The galley slaves rowed all day. They were half-naked. They were whipped, but they weren't ashamed because they were among their own kind. One time, the admiral's daughter took it into her head to visit the galleys. When they saw the beautiful girl walking among them, the galley slaves were ashamed and hated her. And guess what the two galley slaves who escaped the next day did to her, the girl?

Nellie screams off camera.

NOGARO: Have you done, you brute? You wanted to frighten the little lady, eh? Well, you're going to say you're sorry, right now.

Nogaro face to camera, George in profile. Nellie standing, in profile, and the
owner behind her. George gets up on to
his hands again. He sees Nogaro's raised
whip. He smiles, but still with a wicked
look in his eyes.

GEORGE: But of course, miss. I was only
joking. I'm sorry. Very sorry.

Nellie hasn't said a word. She remains
motionless, her face still stiff and
distraught.

George gets up with difficulty. He
wipes each hand on the other and
brushes off his shorts and jacket with
the palm of his hand.

(*Hoarsely*): Give me my bottle of
whisky.

NOGARO: Rikko, a bottle for George.
Put it on my account.

Rikko comes over and hands George a
bottle of whisky. He puts it in his jacket
pocket, turns around, then walks off
without a glance at anyone.

The partition shot square on. The
natives leaning on the partition. George
pushes the little gate and crosses into
the native bar. The natives all turn their
heads to watch him leave. We see him

in the background staggering towards the door. He opens it and disappears.

The owner, Nogaro and Nellie. They are looking silently towards the native bar. Nogaro smiles. The owner turns to Nellie.

OWNER: What was your name again?

NELLIE (*in a colourless voice*): Nellie Dixmier.

The owner claps his hands.

The owner, in profile in the foreground. The sailors sitting to his right, the little man in the bowler hat in front of him. Beyond them, Nellie and Nogaro. Beyond these two, the natives leaning on the partition.

OWNER: Gentlemen, the management would like to present a special act. Miss Nellie Dixmier, the famous crooner, is going to perform some of her most recent numbers.

The sailors applaud.

Shot of Nellie from behind, with hunched shoulders, walking slowly towards the stage at the back.

Dissolve.

*

*

Nellie in her hotel room. She puts on her hat and opens the door. She goes down the stairs and along the corridor. On the right, there is a mirror. On the left, we see the rack of keys and a glass door to the office. Nellie hangs her key on the rack.

HOTEL PROPRIETOR'S VOICE: Miss Dixmier!

Nellie, shot full-length and from behind, opens the office door. Through the glass we see an enormous woman in black, her hair dishevelled. She is sitting knitting in an armchair that has loose covers with a leafy design.

Nellie and the proprietor in the hotel office.

PROPRIETOR: It was, I believe, the tenth when you arrived?

Nellie nods.

It's the nineteenth today.

Nellie remains silent.

Normally, rooms here are paid by the week.

NELLIE: I can't pay at the moment.

The proprietor's already distrustful face hardens.

I work at the 'Mount Everest'. They pay me monthly.

The proprietor's face is hard as stone.

(*Wearily*): All right, I'll ask them for an advance.

PROPRIETOR: Yes, dear girl. They can't deny you that.

The proprietor is all smiles again.

NELLIE: They *can't*? They may well say, 'Ask the proprietor of your hotel to give you credit till the month-end. She can't deny you that.' They're hard people, Miss Flossie. And you too, you're a hard woman . . . Well, I'll do my level best.

She leaves the office.

*

*

In the shantytown:[2] a big fire between the huts. Two women, three men and a child crouching around a sick man lying on a mat on the ground. They are motionless and seem terrified. The sick man is groaning.

Malays come out of the neighbouring huts. One of them loads his possessions and his two children on to a cart and goes off, pulling the cart, after casting a fearful eye over the sick man. Another is pushing a wheelbarrow filled with his few possessions; his children and wife toddle along behind. Others are loading bundles on to their shoulders and leaving. The sick man's parents are left alone to watch over him between the abandoned huts.

Nellie, in the alleyway leading to the nightclub. She is hurrying (as before) and George is there, a dark shape (as before). She walks past him and they exchange glances. George's eyes are full of hatred. Nellie takes a few steps, then makes up her mind to come back towards him.

NELLIE: Why do you hate me? I haven't done anything to you.

George stares at her without replying and turns on his heels. Nellie turns around and watches him disappear into the night.

At Shantytown, by the fire, the death throes of the sick man. He gives a last moan, writhes on his mat, then stiffens, his eyes wide open. He is dead. Then a woman stands up, takes a flaming stick from the fire, lights up the corpse with it, then throws it away. She folds her arms across her chest and begins a wild lamentation.

Nellie and the owner in the middle of the European area of the nightclub.

OWNER: We don't pay in advance, my dear. If you want money, you'll have to earn it.

Nellie shrugs her shoulders, turns her back on him and climbs on to the stage (by a little stairway on the left-hand side). Nellie, shot face to camera, in front of the curtain.

NELLIE: This next song is called 'Malayan Serenade'.

Shot of the Malays all standing around the dead man. The flames of the funeral pyre cast a fantastical light on them (bright light and shadow alternates on each). Softly at first, then louder and louder, they begin to sing a simple, tragic funeral chant.

Singing of the Malays.

Nellie on stage. Her face tragic. She is singing, but we do not hear her voice. Just the shrill, sobbing voice of a woman is heard intermittently against a background of the Malay voices.

Louder singing. An enormous choir, with the sobbing voice of a woman that rises from time to time over the background sound of the men's voices, pronouncing some indistinct words.

The Malays singing and dancing on the spot around the dead man.

George staggering in an alleyway. Seen face to camera, looking exhausted and tragic. He comes up to the windows of the 'Mount Everest' and presses his face to the pane. Through it, we see Nellie singing at the back of the club. Then he turns away and leaves.

The bottle floating, tossed by furious waves.

Nellie singing. This time, she is the one heard and the Malays' singing serves as a background.

She bows. Weak applause. The Malays' singing stops abruptly.

The door to the European bar, seen from the inside. The bearded man and the tall man with the moustache enter, followed by two girls in loud, vulgar, dresses—clearly high-class tarts. The two men standing still against the wall, waiting for the music to stop before taking their seats. In the doorway, the two women, laughing.

The bearded man looks all around. Then he looks towards the stage. He

The singing of the Malays, louder.

The singing of the Malays, like an enormous breaking wave. The woman's voice sings, more distinctly, 'In the Night of his Pride!'

Singing of the Malays.

NELLIE: *In the dark night,*
In the night of his pride.

A ritornello from guitar and piano brings Nellie's song to an end.

tugs at the other man's sleeve. The man with the moustache looks in the direction in which the bearded man is nodding. His face registers astonishment and amusement.

The owner dashes up to meet them, rubbing his hands.

The four in profile, full-length, with the owner.

A table with four chairs. They sit.

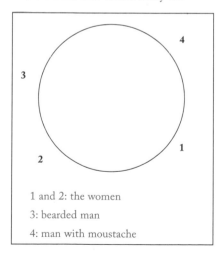

1 and 2: the women
3: bearded man
4: man with moustache

MAN WITH MOUSTACHE: No kidding!

OWNER: A good table?
BEARDED MAN: Yes, that one at the back. We'll be fine there.

Tell me, what's your singer called?
OWNER: Nellie Dixmier.
MAN WITH MOUSTACHE: Send her over. Tell her we'll stand her a drink.
FIRST TART: Hey, but what are *we* here for? If you've had enough of us, you've only got to say so.
MAN WITH MOUSTACHE: Don't you worry. We're going to have a bit of fun.

Shot of Nogaro at another table, playing patience. From time to time he looks up and casts a puzzled glance in their direction.

The table, the four of them seated, from right to left: the two women shot from behind, the bearded man in profile and the man with the moustache face to camera.

Same shot. The two women are looking at the wine list. The two men have turned to face the back. In the background, we see Nellie coming towards them.

ONE OF THE WOMEN (*from behind, looking up*): Darling, will you order us some champagne?

Same shot. Nellie between the two men who part to make room for her.

NELLIE: You want to talk to me?

She recognizes them. Clearly, this is not a pleasant encounter for her. The man with the moustache, slouching deep in his armchair, holds out his hand to her without getting up.

MAN WITH MOUSTACHE: Hello, baby. Do you recognize me? This is a turn-up, eh?

Nellie shakes his hand. He turns to the two tarts.

This is a lady we met on the bus. Oh

and here's Fred. Recognize him too?

Nellie shakes the hand of Fred, who doesn't get up either.

The tarts laugh.

FRED: We were hot that day. God, we were hot!

FIRST TART: Not hot enough to get you slim, pops!

MAN WITH MOUSTACHE: Have a drink with us, Baby. Waiter!

Rikko appears on the right.

Bring a chair. And then two bottles of Lanson, well iced!

The waiter brings an armchair. Nellie sits down.

(Doing the introductions): Rosita, Mercedes and Baby. Three little good-time girls.

The waiter brings the glasses and serves the champagne.

(To the two tarts): I kept looking at her and saying to myself, she is decidedly well-stacked, she is. She kept getting out of the bus, getting back in, wiggling about. I could see right to the top of her legs through her dress. God, I was sweating. But I said to myself, calm down Mac, she's with a bloke. She's not for the likes of you. And then . . . isn't that life all over? Ha, ha, ha. Isn't that just the way it

On him.

On Fred.

On Mac.

Fred and the tart beside him (Fred in profile, the tart from behind).

She puts her arms around his neck and strokes his beard.

The tarts from behind, Fred in profile, Nellie face to camera, Mac in three-quarter view. Nellie seems in agony.

Mac raises his glass. Nellie has a hunted look about her, then slowly raises her glass.

goes? (*To Fred*) What do you say to that?'

FRED: I say, we were hot that day! God, we were hot!

Laughter.

MAC: There you are. Forgive him. He's never been able to appreciate the fairer sex.

SECOND TART: He's in love with his beard. Isn't that right, pops? You're in love with that fine, silky beard of yours. Bah, you old madman.

MAC: So, a toast, baby?

To the bus from Santareya! And no hard feelings, baby.

FIRST TART: Why do you say, 'No hard feelings'?

MAC: 'Cos she cost me a hundred pounds!

NELLIE (*almost involuntarily*): I cost you . . . ?

MAC: Ask Fred. I had a meeting with a Shanghai industrialist who was waiting here to do some business. But this little girl spotted a fine figure of a Malay on the road and got him up on the bus. Only the Malay had typhus, so we were all banged up in hospital, quarantined, and the man from Shanghai left on the *São Paulo* without waiting for me. Ha, ha, ha. That's the way it goes! That's the way it goes!

(*Turning round to the tarts*): Hey, kids, don't you think Baby owes me some compensation?

THE TWO TARTS: Yes, yes. A night of passion.

MAC: There you are, Baby. It was their idea. A night of passion. Twelve hours in seventh heaven, Malay style, Tibetan style, Chinese . . . Indochinese . . . What do you say to that, Baby?

He chucks her under the chin. She pulls away in disgust. Mac is still smiling, but he has a nasty look about him.

You're certainly a cocky little thing. Do I disgust you? Or is it only Malays that you like?

Nellie has calmed down. She tries to be sweet and almost humble.

NELLIE: Excuse me, but I'm not really in the mood for fun. That bus left some unpleasant memories.

He pulls her violently to him.

MAC: That's just it, darling. You've got to forget them, forget them. Look, sit up on my lap here. We'll drown those memories in sensual delight.

Nellie pulls away and stands up.

NELLIE: Leave me alone. Can't you leave me? Look, you're all together, having a good time and I'm not pretty, young or really much fun. I don't see what you want with me.

Mac looks at her angrily.

MAC: You're right, baby. You can go, we won't keep you. We don't need a wet blanket. Do you know why she's pulling that face, kids? It's 'cos the bitch did her bloke in.

Nellie suddenly pales and gazes at him, wide-eyed.

NELLIE: Shut your mouth! That's not true! It's not true!

MAC: Oh, isn't it? Wasn't it the Malay who infected him? And didn't he die in the hospital because of what you did?

A distraught Nellie picks up a champagne glass from the table and throws it in his face. The glass smashes. Mac is soaked and his cheek is bleeding. He jumps up suddenly.

Oh, you bitch!

Shot of the bearded man who has begun hurriedly chewing his beard.

On Mac. He has grabbed Nellie by the shoulder and raises his hand.

The European bar. The five of them in the middle. Nogaro sitting at a table on the left. On the right, the owner runs up limping. Nogaro gets up to intervene but the owner is there first. With a honeyed smile, he halts Mac's hand in mid-flight.

Nellie hasn't moved. Her arms are by her sides, her head is erect and she has a severe look about her.

OWNER: I entirely understand how angry you are, sir. And I can assure you the young lady will be dismissed this very evening. But I can have no scandal in my establishment. The police are very strict. We would be forced to close.

MAC: All right. Take a good look at me, because it'll be a very long time before you see us again. Come on, kids, we're going to the 'Parrot Club'. Come on, Fred.

The two tarts have got up. Fred, still sitting in his armchair, crimson-faced and with tears in his eyes, coughs.

FIRST TART: What's the matter, pops?

FRED: I'm choking . . . choking on my beard.

The tarts laugh. One of them lifts him up and stands him on his feet. The other slaps him on the back as she pulls him along. Mac has left ahead of them with a mean look in his eyes.

The owner and Nellie.

OWNER: I want a word with you in a moment, Nellie.

At the door, Mac turns around.

MAC (*to Owner*): I trust you won't be charging us for those bottles of champagne. You at least owe me that.

*

*

The Malays at Shantytown. They put the body on a stretcher and light torches from the fire. Two men load the stretcher on to their shoulders and set off down the road, followed by the other Malays who are singing.

Malayan singing.

The porters. The first shot head-and-shoulders, the body, then the second shot from the waist up, walking. At times they are lit, at times in half-darkness. We see the dancing flames of the torches.

Malayan lament.

The Malays on the road. On their way they pass a man, who turns and looks back at them. It is George.

George, from behind, walking up towards Shantytown.

George, from behind, entering his cabin, stooping over the lock. The dog jumps all around him. George goes in. The dog wants to come in too, but George slams the door on it. Whining

Door slams sharply shut.

Whining of the dog.

of the dog, which sniffs at the bottom of the door.

George in his cabin. He strikes a match and lights a candle on the table. The interior is illuminated. A chair at a table, a picture of George on the wall. George pulls a bottle of whisky from his jacket pocket. He unscrews the top with his teeth. He is about to drink but stops in his tracks and looks up at the picture.

GEORGE: It vexes you to see me drink, eh? You bastard! You didn't drink, did you? Too well brought up for that. You watched the drunks with that sad look of yours. It hurt you that men could fall so low. Well, sod you! You make me sick.

He stands up and turns the picture to the wall. He sits down again, smiles with delight and starts drinking again.

The 'Mount Everest' club. It is empty. The owner and Rikko in the European section, shot full-length near the bar.

OWNER: You can turn off the lights and close up, Rikko. No one else is coming tonight. I'm going upstairs to have a word with Nellie.

RIKKO: Will you be coming back down, boss?

OWNER: No.

He moves off to the right.

Nellie in her dressing room, sitting in front of the mirror at her make-up table. Shot full-length in profile, we also see her in the mirror. She is finishing removing her make-up. There are photographs of naked women on the walls, together with graffiti. The dressing room is bare and gloomy; it has a run-down look. A knock at the door.

NELLIE: Come in.

The owner comes in and stands in front of her. He is standing at an angle to the camera, in profile, in front of Nellie. He folds his arms across his chest.

OWNER: Right, clear off. I don't want to see you again.

NELLIE: Listen, boss. That bloke insulted me . . .

OWNER: So what? What do I pay you for if it isn't to be insulted by the customers? You don't think I hired you for your voice, do you?

Nellie is on her feet. She gives him a cold stare.

NELLIE: It so happens that I did.

OWNER: Oh, that's enough of that.

Don't come the great artiste with me.
I hired you. You don't fit the bill. I'm
firing you. That's all there is to it.

Nellie looks at him anxiously, but controls her emotions. She takes her hat and puts it on.

But she doesn't go. She waits.

NELLIE: All right, I'm going.

OWNER: What are you waiting for?

NELLIE: To be paid. I may not fit the bill, but I've sung here for six days.

The owner gives a wicked laugh.

OWNER: That's a good one. What about the bottles of champagne your man didn't pay for? Who's going to pay me back for those? They come to almost twice what I owe you. It's good of me not to make you pay the difference.

Nellie is pale with anger.

NELLIE: You should have made him pay. That's not my problem.

OWNER: Oh, that's brilliant. We're on to reasoned argument now, are we? How much longer are you intending to get on my nerves, you little tart?

He goes to the dressing-room door and opens it.

You'll kindly shut your trap and get out of here, unless you want me to help you along with a kick up the backside.

Nellie is livid. Her hands are trembling with fury. But she speaks coldly, not raising her voice.

NELLIE: It's because I'm all alone that you dare speak to me like that. If I had a man, you'd mind what you said. You'd be too scared he might come and give you what for, you puny little runt. You little creep. You're bitter and twisted because you're a cripple, and you take it out on the weak. But you've made a mistake with me, because I'm not weak. And I'm telling you to your face that you're a coward and a swine.

The owner comes towards her.

OWNER: Say that again, honey.

NELLIE: A coward and a swine.

OWNER: Right! On your way!

He slaps her with all his might. Nellie is dumbfounded for a moment, then hurls herself at him kicking and scratching. He tries to avoid her and falls. He grabs her leg and tries to pull her down too. She grabs the lamp from the table and hits him on the head. He falls back. She gazes at him, terror-stricken, dropping the lamp, which breaks. The light goes out in the dressing room. The scene is lit only by the light from the corridor streaming through the wide-open door. Nellie stoops down, cradles his head in her hands, then draws them back covered in blood. She recoils in horror, putting one hand to her face. She walks out backwards into the corridor. The camera is placed in the darkened room. Nellie has receded into the distance, and is seen beneath the ceiling light in the corridor. We can see that she has smeared her face with blood. She seems distraught.

RIKKO'S VOICE: What's going on, boss? Do you need me?

The corridor. Nellie is listening anxiously, holding her breath. Not a sound. Rikko must have decided not to come up. She runs off on tiptoe and opens a window in the corridor. We see an outside staircase of the kind found on American buildings. She climbs out of the window.

Nellie in the street. She runs past the camera. Nellie seen from behind, running towards the end of the street. At the end of the street is a policeman crossing the road. Nellie stops, turns around and runs off in the opposite direction. She seems on the verge of madness.

Another street. Nellie suddenly comes out into it. She seems a little calmer. She is coming towards the camera, not running. Suddenly, two blasts on a whistle are heard in the night. Nellie, full-length, quite close to the camera. Her face changes. She looks distraught once more and starts running again.

Two long blasts on a whistle.

*

*

On the road, outside the town. The natives walking, carrying the stretcher. Torches and singing. They come towards the camera.

Malayan singing.

On the road, but in the other direction (moving away from the camera), Nellie running and stumbling.

Nellie gasping for breath.
Malayan singing.

The Malays.

Nellie.

George, in profile, sitting at his table, looking glassy-eyed and dull-witted.

Nellie running.

Malayan singing in the far distance.
Nellie's panting for breath.
The Malayan singing comes nearer.

She stumbles and falls by the roadside.

Nellie exhausted, stretched out at the roadside, with the procession in the distance, the light of their torches visible in the darkness.

Ditto.

The procession passes, the torches lighting up Nellie's prostrate body. The Malays pass by the camera in close-up without seeing her and disappear.

Nellie on the dark road. She struggles to her feet and begins running.

Sound of a car in the distance. Shot of the approaching car behind Nellie. Nellie caught in the car's headlights. She is running (shot from behind) in the light, her shadow stretching out before her. She turns around in panic, jumps right off the road and runs across the fields.

Nellie walking between the huts of Shantytown.

Close-up of her exhausted face.

Nellie near George's cabin. She limps past the cabin and passes on beyond. A weak light shows through the old newspapers that serve as the cabin's windows. At this point, George's dog comes out of the night and sets upon her, growling. Nellie (still being shot from behind) steps back. The dog comes forward. She stoops down, picks up a stone and throws it at him. The dog runs off but soon comes back again, growling. Nellie now seen in profile.

Shot of Nellie looking at her hand, which has only one stone left, then the dog. She throws her stone at him, then turns around and runs up to George's cabin with the dog at her heels. She throws open the door of the cabin, runs inside and slams the door on the dog.

Nellie face to camera, her back against the door she has just shut. Dumbfounded, she stares at George (out of shot).

On George. He has drunk half his bottle. He is sitting at the table with his legs turned towards Nellie. He stares at her, maliciously, but unsurprised.

GEORGE: So you've come to pay me a little visit. That's nice, that is.

Nellie face to camera. She looks at him for a moment without replying, then turns around, opens the door and is about to dash out. Barking of the dog, which we see spring towards her. Nellie hurriedly closes the door again and turns round to George.

On George.

He gets up and comes towards Nellie.

Nellie and George.

He reaches out his hand and takes the chair by its back.

He sits astride the chair, facing its back.

George leans over to the table and picks up the bottle.

She takes the bottle and drinks straight from it. He gives an unpleasant laugh.

She moves towards the table. She has regained her strength.

NELLIE (*imperiously*): I want to leave.

GEORGE: I'm not stopping you.

NELLIE: Send the dog away.

GEORGE: Why should I do that?

A seat?

NELLIE: No.

GEORGE: As you wish. Excuse me if I sit down. A drop of whisky? You look like you need it.

NELLIE: No . . . er, yes. You're right, I need it. Pour me one.

GEORGE: Well now, I don't have a glass. You'll have to drink straight from the bottle. Like me.

NELLIE: I don't mind.

George: face to camera. Nellie puts the bottle on the table. She herself sits on the corner of the table, her legs dangling.

Are you going to let me go?

GEORGE: Did I ask you to come?

A pause. Nellie swings her legs to and fro. George looks at her, his eyes sparkling.

Remember the admiral's daughter?

NELLIE (*standing up to him*): I remember everything. You're despicable. Cowardly to men and fresh with women. The works.

GEORGE: I didn't tell you what they did to her, the two escaped convicts?

NELLIE: No, you got a thrashing that interrupted your story.

GEORGE: Well, I'll tell you now.

NELLIE: No need. I can quite imagine.

George reaches out to take the bottle of whisky. Nellie whisks it out of his reach.

Oh, no you don't! You're not gonna get plastered so you can build up the nerve to jump me. You can do that sober—if you dare?

George lets his arm fall. He examines Nellie's hand.

GEORGE: Have you been bleeding a pig tonight?

Nellie laughs in his face.

Nellie jumps off the table. On Nellie, head and shoulders.

NELLIE: What if I have?

GEORGE: What if you have? Do you know what I do for a living?

NELLIE: Yes, you're an exotic dancer. I've had an opportunity to appreciate your talents.

GEORGE: I'm also a copper's nark.

NELLIE: Ah? (*Pulls herself together*) Can't say I'm surprised. You look the type.

GEORGE (*unaffected by the remark*): I know you sang tonight. Two hours later, you're out of town with blood all over your hands and face. You haven't had time to go back to your hotel and, anyway, you're still wearing the evening dress you use for your act. You did the dirty deed at the 'Mount Everest'. You've either bumped off Nogaro or the boss. But it can't be Nogaro—he's too much of a handful for you.

NELLIE: You should know about that.

GEORGE: Logically, then, you must have bumped off the boss. Is that it?

Nellie goes over to him.

NELLIE: Since you're the great detective, I don't know why you're asking me.

GEORGE: Ah! You've done the boss in . . . Well, you could have chosen worse.

NELLIE: That's enough, you filthy grass. Go on. Go get your reward money. Hurry up, don't waste time with wisecracks.

GEORGE: Hold on. There's no big rush. You had a laugh at me the other night. Surely I can have a bit of fun with you today.

He gets up too. He tries to take the bottle of whisky. She prevents him by hanging on to his arm.

NELLIE: No, no. That would be too easy. Go and grass on me sober.

George laughing, while she hangs on to his arm.

GEORGE: Here she is, the admiral's daughter. She's come to pay me a little visit. I gave you a good laugh, eh? And now I only have to lift my little finger . . .

As he speaks, he eases his way towards the bottle of whisky. He is on the point of grabbing it.

Nellie sweeps the bottle away with her hand. It falls on the floor and breaks.

George raises his hand to her.

NELLIE (*triumphant*): Ha!

GEORGE: Bloody bitch!

A silence.

He slowly lowers his hand. He looks at the ground.

The broken whisky bottle.

The liquid runs out and on to the floor.

On George.

George and Nellie. A pause. He looks at Nellie's hands.

GEORGE: Never fear. I shan't hit you. I've better things to do. Go and wash your hands for God's sake!

NELLIE: What's the good of that now?

GEORGE: Yes, of course. You must have left your calling card. Blood on the walls, a dozen fingerprints and hairpins near the body. A woman's crime, eh? Where did you kill him?

NELLIE: In my dressing room.

GEORGE: Perfect. And it didn't occur to you to drag the body outside?

A pause.

GEORGE: Are you going to wash your hands?

He grabs her by the shoulders and drags her to the barrel. He plunges her hands into it and rubs them.

Like that. And now your face! What a mess.

He takes her by the neck. She struggles, but he pushes her face down into the barrel. She comes up, half-suffocated, her hair soaking and water dripping down her cheeks. She pulls a comical face. He laughs.

He takes an old rag down from above the barrel and rubs her cheeks roughly.

What a sight! Let's get that blood off.

That's all right now. You go home. I'll sort this out.

NELLIE: What?

GEORGE: I said I'll sort it out. I'm going to go over there and clean up the mess you've left.

NELLIE: What's got into you? You're an informer, do your job. Did I ask for your help?

On George. He is looking at her coldly.

GEORGE (*severely*): That's just it, darling. It's because you didn't ask anything of me. It can't be much fun to be in the debt of a drunkard, a coward and a copper's nark. Off with you! Go home, and try and get some sleep. And if you wonder sometimes why I did this for you, I don't imagine you'll enjoy the answer you come up with. Goodbye.

On the two of them.

He goes to the door. George shot from behind. Nellie watches him leave. As he's about to open the door, she calls him back.

NELLIE: Hey!

He turns around.

Her proud bearing is gone.

What about . . . er, the dog?

GEORGE (*laughing*): That's women all over! You play the tough guy with men, but dogs are something different. It's all right. I'll take him with me.

He opens the door and whistles. The dog barks. He closes the door behind him.

Nellie, full-length from behind, her head turned towards the door.

Nellie turns around. She seems to be emerging from a dream. She looks around her. She opens the drawers in the table. They are empty. She looks up at the photograph that has been turned to the wall. She turns it round the right way and gazes at it for a moment. Then she blows out the candle, opens the door and goes out too.

We hear the barking of a dog outside growing fainter.

*

*

Outside the 'Mount Everest' club by night. George pushes gently at the windows with his hand, but they do not give way.

The street. George follows it round.

The camera follows him. He turns into an alleyway behind the club, goes over to a metal ladder (the one Nellie came down) and begins to climb.

The corridor, unlit. The open window makes a square of light against the darkness of the corridor. Shot of George climbing over the window rail. He jumps noiselessly into the corridor, strikes a match and moves along.

Outside Nellie's dressing room. The door is still open. Another match. A smashed lamp on the carpet, but no corpse.

George's face, disconcerted, seen in the light of the match flame.

He goes out into the corridor. At the end of it, there is a ray of light coming from under a door. George creeps up stealthily and puts his eye to the keyhole.

The keyhole framing the nightclub owner, his head wrapped in an enormous bandage, mournfully contemplating his image in a mirror.

George's face in the half-darkness. He begins to chuckle silently.

Dissolve.

*   *

Next morning at the Governor's Palace. The Governor seated at his desk. He is a very slender man of about 65 years, with white hair, wrinkles and hollow eyes. Around his desk, in a semi-circle from right to left, are the director of the hospital, Drs Thomas, Sleep, Starrett and Mountain, the police chief in uniform and two or three notables.

The Governor is standing?[3]

GOVERNOR: Take a seat, gentlemen. You all know each other, I take it?

They mutely nod assent. A few handshakes. They sit. The Governor is face to camera, the doctors are shot in three-quarter view and in profile, the police chief from behind and the other advisors in profile on the left.

The Governor sits down.

I don't need to explain the situation to you. It is, I fear, grave. How many cases of typhus have there been at the hospital, Smith?

HOSPITAL DIRECTOR: About a hundred up to this point. But you know, as I do, Governor, that the natives are reluctant to be treated by us. I should think there's three times that amount of serious cases in Shantytown and the dock area.

The police chief, shot full-length and in profile.

POLICE CHIEF: I very much fear you're right. I was told this morning of a suspicious death in Shantytown. Last night, there was a torchlit funeral. More seriously, people have begun to move out. The huts are emptying, the natives have taken to the roads, heading in every direction.

On the Governor.

GOVERNOR: You are to give orders that all those who've left are to be rounded up and sent back. The first thing we have to do is stop the panic. And, anyway, where can they go? There's 400 miles of desert out there. (*To the doctors*) The European districts aren't affected, are they?

On Dr Thomas.

DR THOMAS. Not yet.

All of them. The Governor, face to camera.

GOVERNOR: Good. Well, there's still plenty of hope. Only, we must act quickly. The whole population needs to be vaccinated within the next 48 hours. Smith, is there enough vaccine?

SMITH: It's difficult to say. We sent quite a lot to Santareya at the beginning of last month. I imagine what's left will be enough, but only just. We'll have to be very sparing with it.

On one of the notables, from the left.

On Starrett.

On all of them, Starrett in profile.

GOVERNOR: Right. I'm counting on you.

DR STARRETT: And how are we going to get the natives to come and be vaccinated? You know what happened at Santareya. They all cleared off. They loathe the vaccine. They say it's against their religion and that a man's blood must remain pure. And then I think they're mostly scared witless of injections.

NOTABLE: They'll have to be forced to come. That's all there is to it.

DR STARRETT: That's easy to say. But how can we check they haven't been vaccinated? There's no register of persons, and they all have the same names. If we gave everyone we picked up in the street a jab, there's a chance we'd do the same ones four or five times. Do you see? These poor fellows will die on us. And, at that rate, the vaccine won't last long either, I can assure you.

NOTABLE: Well, we can ask them, can't we? They've got tongues in their heads.

DR STARRETT: The very idea! They'll all tell you they've been done.

The Governor raises his hand.

GOVERNOR: Gentlemen, I've already thought of all this and here is what I propose. We're going to ask for army support and organize a systematic round-up of all the natives in the northern and southern districts. I'll ask the Europeans to take their Malayan servants to the hospital. And I've had vaccination certificates prepared. We'll issue them to all the natives who've received a jab. After that, any native who doesn't have one of these certificates will be immediately taken to the hospital and you'll vaccinate him as a matter of course. Are you in agreement?

A pause. Then on the police chief, face to camera.

POLICE CHIEF: These vaccination certificates . . . When all's said and done, they'll be like bearer cheques?

On the Governor.

GOVERNOR: Exactly.

The Governor and the police chief, both in profile.

POLICE CHIEF: Hum! . . . The point is that bearer cheques are negotiable.

The Governor shrugs his shoulders.

GOVERNOR: I know, but I can't see any better way.

*

*

Shantytown. Intense, chaotic activity. Natives are piling their belongings on carts, wheelbarrows or their backs and are starting to leave. The camera follows some of them on the road. We see the beginnings of the exodus from a distance: long lines of Malays leaving in silence.

George face to camera, full-length, in a square in the town. He comes towards the camera. He is not slouching as much as before and his gaze is more lively.

On the square, the facade of Nellie's hotel. Above the door, we read 'Hotel Victoria'. George goes into the hotel.

In the proprietor's office. The proprietor in profile, full-length, in her armchair. She is knitting. The glass door is at the back, a little to the left. There is a knock and she looks up. We see George's face through the pane.

PROPRIETOR: What do you want?

George opens the door.

GEORGE: Miss Nellie Dixmier.

PROPRIETOR: Don't come in. You'll bring me your lice and that's likely to be dangerous at the moment. What do you want with the Dixmier woman?

GEORGE: I want to speak to her.

PROPRIETOR: Stay out there. I don't want you going up into the rooms looking such a fright. I'll call her.

She heaves herself out of the chair and goes to the door. George moves aside to let her pass.

The proprietor in the hotel yard (a dark, square yard), shot full-length from behind, her head raised. Above her, facing the camera, a high wall with many windows.

Miss Dixmier! Miss Dixmier!

A window opens on the third floor. Nellie appears in her dressing gown, looking very pale and worried.

NELLIE: What is it?

PROPRIETOR: Come down! There's someone asking for you.

Nellie is afraid.

NELLIE: Who is it? Who's asking for me?

PROPRIETOR: You'll see. He's no better than he should be.

Nellie closes the window again. The proprietor from behind, going back in.

George alone in the corridor at the foot of the staircase. He goes over to a mirror and takes a long look at himself. George from behind. We see his image facing us in the mirror. The proprietor approaches (in profile). He turns around suddenly.

George and the proprietor in profile, face to face. George looks at her.

GEORGE: You're right, I do look a fright. Give me a pencil.

She takes a pencil from her apron pocket and hands it to him. George has taken a crumpled piece of paper from his pocket.

George from behind, seen from above. We see him writing: we see his forearm, hand, the pencil and the paper. He writes: 'The owner of the Mount Everest is fit and well.'

He hands the pencil and paper to the hotel proprietor.

Here. Thank you. Give her this from me.

PROPRIETOR: She's on her way down.

GEORGE: I know. But I don't want to give her a fright, do I? Looking the way I do.

He waves a vague hand towards her, turns around and leaves.

The proprietor, left there alone, unfolds the paper, reads it and folds it again. The proprietor face to camera, at the foot of the stairs. Behind her we see the staircase rising into the half-darkness. Nellie appears on the stairs. She is dressed, but bare-headed.

The owner turns round. We see her from behind.

NELLIE (*nervously*): Where is he?

PROPRIETOR: He's gone.

NELLIE: Was it . . . someone from the police?

PROPRIETOR (*distrustful and surprised*): From the police? It was a Malay. He left this for you.

Nellie comes down a few steps. The proprietor hands her the note. She unfolds it and reads it. She begins to laugh nervously, a laugh verging on nervous collapse. She comes down the stairs, still laughing, walks past the proprietor, who stares after her, and then turns round to look back at her.

At the foot of the stairs, the proprietor in profile. Nellie turning her back to her and walking, in profile. The proprietor grabs her arm and spins her round. Nellie and the proprietor in profile, full-length, face to face.

Nellie is still laughing.

So, my dear, did you ask your boss for money?

NELLIE: Oh, yes! Oh, yes! I asked him for money.

PROPRIETOR (*more friendly*): And?

NELLIE (*laughing*): And . . . And he threw me out. I haven't a penny, dear lady. I'm out of a job.

On the proprietor, quaking with indignation. She opens her mouth to speak.

(*Laughing*): I get it, dear lady. I get it. I'm on my way.

She turns round and walks off down the corridor. The proprietor is speechless with fury.

The corridor, with the office on the right. Facing the camera, in the background, the open hotel entrance. The proprietor, shot from behind, is in the foreground. Nellie, from behind, leaving by the main door. When she is outside, the proprietor recovers her breath and rushes towards the door.

Nellie, face to camera, on the square, with the proprietor, face-on, behind her in the hotel doorway. She shouts.

PROPRIETOR: She's got a cheek, that one! Don't ever set foot in here again or I'll have the police on you. And I'm keeping your cases until you've paid your bill.

Nellie doesn't turn round and doesn't seem to hear. She walks on mechanically, with a vague, distraught air.

*

*

The interior of the 'Mount Everest'. A few natives are drinking in the native bar. In the European bar all the chairs are on the tables, except at one where Nogaro is playing patience. Rikko is sluicing down the floor. The owner, with his head bandaged, is limping around the room. Nogaro looks at him and starts to laugh. The owner stops and gives him a nasty look.

OWNER: What's with you?

NOGARO: She sorted you out OK!

OWNER: Give me a break.

Nogaro shuffles the cards and lays them out on the table.

NOGARO: You see, it's always the same.

The owner shrugs his shoulders and
turns his back on him. A pause.

The owner (over his shoulder).

The owner turns around sharply.

The owner comes and sits down.

Nogaro and the owner. Nogaro goes on
playing patience as he speaks.

She wasn't nice to the customers. You
weren't nice to her. She wasn't nice to
you. People are never nice enough to
each other.

Mercutio!

OWNER: What is it this time?'

NOGARO: *I'll* be nice to you. Do you
want to make 50 bucks?

OWNER: What do I have to do?

NOGARO: Come and sit down next to
me.

You know they're going to vaccinate
all the Malays?

OWNER: Yes.

NOGARO: But the Malays don't like it.

OWNER: So what?

NOGARO: They'll be given vaccination
cards, one apiece, without any names
on.

OWNER: How do you know that?

NOGARO: I just do.

OWNER: And what the hell has that to
do with me?

On Nogaro.

NOGARO: There are Malays who are rich. They'd give a lot not to have to have the jab.

OWNER: And?

NOGARO: And there's also poor Malays. They'd sell their grandmothers for something to eat. Suppose we buy the certificates from the poor Malays and sell them on to the rich ones? Everybody's happy and we'll have been nice to everyone. What do you say?

On the two. The owner is tempted, but anxious.

OWNER: I say, it's quite risky.

NOGARO (*affectionately*): Silly boy! Do you think we're going to do it ourselves? The thing is to find someone who's known by the natives, someone they like. There's nothing like keeping it in the family. Now I come to think of it, someone like George . . .

The offices of the Consulate of . . . Nellie standing at a counter window. She is shot in profile and we see a curly-haired clerk on the other side of the window.

NELLIE: I thought the Consulate was repatriating the destitute.

CLERK: Do you have a certificate of destitution?

NELLIE: I can get one.

CLERK: It takes 10 days to obtain a certificate.

NELLIE: I'll try to hold out for 10 days.

CLERK: But you'd be better off looking for work. Because even if you had a certificate, we couldn't send you home.

NELLIE: Why not?

CLERK: Because it'll be many a long day before another ship calls in at Ottawee. We're quarantined on account of the typhus.

NELLIE: So I shan't be able to go back to Europe? I'm going to be here a long time?

Well, where can I find work?

The clerk motions to suggest that he doesn't know.

CLERK: Work? There's none to be had, miss. If the port's not working, there'll soon be 20,000 unemployed.

NELLIE: But you said . . .

CLERK: I told you to look for work. I didn't say you'd find any.

NELLIE: So, what's to become of me?

CLERK: That I can't say. Come and see us in a few days' time. We may have something.

NELLIE (*weakly*): Thank you. I'll see what I can find.

CLERK: Goodbye, miss. Keep your pecker up.

Nellie nods to the clerk and goes out slowly.

Nellie face to camera, head and shoulders. She seems totally at a loss.

Full-length shot, face to camera, of George in the street outside the 'Mount Everest'. He is walking limply again. But he has cast off his hazy look. He is hard-faced and gloomy. He enters by the door to the native bar.

The native area. George goes in and sits at a table, turning his back on the European bar.

GEORGE: A bottle of whisky. I can pay for it.

On the other side of the partition, the owner and Nogaro looking at—and nudging—each other.

NOGARO: *You* go. He must be mad at me after the other night.

The owner gets up and comes towards the camera.

George sitting. The owner comes up to him from behind. George in the foreground, face to camera, and the owner behind him. He puts a hand on George's shoulder.

George turns his head slowly and gives him a cold stare.

He takes a chair and makes to sit down.

Nellie wandering the streets, distraught. Full-length shot, face to camera. A native coming out of a Malayan house suddenly blocks her way. He comes out carrying a stretcher. A sick man on the stretcher. Another native follows, carrying the rear shafts of the stretcher. Nellie looks at them, then goes on her way again. Nellie in profile. She tries to cross the street, but is forced to wait because natives go by pulling carts behind them with all their possessions and, in many cases, children on them. She eventually manages to cross and goes into a sidestreet at random. Shot in the foreground, from behind. Two natives pass in front of her, carrying a stretcher. She stops and stares after

OWNER: The bottle's on the house. A gift from me.

GEORGE: What are you after?

OWNER: Wait a second. I'll get a chair and fill you in.

them (turning her head) and then sets off again a little more quickly.

She is walking in the crowd. A woman is crying, standing in the middle of four others, chattering away in Malayan. Nellie moves towards the group.

Nellie, face to camera, watching the weeping woman with a strange, surprised, almost blind gaze. (Two women in profile, the one crying is shot from behind, her shoulders are shaking convulsively—both from the waist up).

A NATIVE WOMAN (*to Nellie, speaking English with difficulty*): Her little boy is sick. She thinks he has the typhus.

Nellie shudders. She rummages in her bag and brings out a handful of change—the last of her money.

NELLIE: That's all I have. That will help you to get treatment for him.

In a dark, native bedroom. A ray of sunshine coming through the shutters, patches of sunlight on the floor. A thin, half-naked adolescent leaning over his mother. He speaks to her in Malayan, but she doesn't reply. He touches her, stares at her with terror in his eyes and suddenly jumps to his feet shouting.

ADOLESCENT: Typhus!

The adolescent, shot face to camera, in the street, running and shouting.

Typhus!

Nellie, shot face to camera, walking heavily, unrelentingly, lifelessly.

The adolescent running in a public square.

As he passes, natives grouping together and speaking in Malayan.

Typhus!

Nellie, in profile, walking.

The word 'typhus' keeps recurring in their conversation.

We hear the word 'typhus' in the distance. At first softly, then louder and louder.

The adolescent comes out into the street where Nellie is walking. He shouts and comes towards her.

Close-up of the adolescent's face, his mouth open.

Nellie and the adolescent. He goes by her, jostling her almost, and runs off wild-eyed.

ADOLESCENT: TYPHUS!

A crowd gathers by Nellie.

The word 'typhus' recurring.

*

*

George and the owner. Same position as before. George has a bottle of whisky.

GEORGE: Right. I'll have a think about it. Leave me alone. I'm going to have a drink. That'll clear my mind.

The proprietor gets up, looks at him for a moment, then goes off. George, left alone, pours himself a drink. It is clear he has decided to get drunk. He already has his glassy stare and hazy expression. He drinks.

Nellie appears in a street, in profile, passes in front of the camera, walks on, with the camera viewing her from behind, and stops dead.

Nellie from behind, standing still against a wall. The alleyway has no pavement. By her a horse-drawn cart has stopped. Corpses covered up with cloth are laid out on stretchers in the cart. A man standing on the cart, looking up. A stretcher with a covered corpse on it is let down from the fourth floor using two ropes. Nellie stands and watches. When the stretcher reaches the level of the cart and the driver, who is standing, pulls it towards him, she lets out a scream, turns around and begins walking very quickly—in fact, almost running—in the opposite direction.

Nellie, face to camera, almost running. The camera retreats as she advances.

A relentless whispering in her ears (in time with her steps): 'Typhus! Typhus! Typhus!'

The street outside the 'Mount Everest' club. The 'Mount Everest', at the doorway to the European bar. Nellie arrives, shot face to camera, almost running. She sees the sign, hesitates a moment and then enters.

The bar, from the inside. At the back, Rikko is washing the floor. On the right, Nogaro is playing patience. The owner, shot face to camera, to the left of the partition and, on the far left, on the other side of the partition, George who is visibly drunk.

Nellie, shot from behind, walking diagonally from right to left towards the owner. Nogaro looks up, smiles and smacks his lips, then goes back to his game of patience.

The partition: George on the other side of it. He has seen Nellie. He clenches his fists and shakes his head, making a palpable effort to sober up. Without success. He tries to stand, but falls back into his chair.

In the foreground Nellie, shot in profile. The owner shot face to camera. He is quaking with anger and astonishment. He tries to speak, but cannot. Nellie stops in front of him.

NELLIE: I haven't a penny to my name and I won't stand on my dignity any more. I want to go back to Europe. I don't want to die here. I'll do anything to get back. I've come to ask you to forgive me. Take me back, I'll do what you want.

On George. He has finally managed to stand up, his eyes flashing with anger.

The owner, crimson with fury, still dumbstruck, can only point Nellie to the door.

Please, please. I'll be there for the customers.

The owner continues to point to the exit. She waits a moment, then turns around and walks towards the door. Nogaro watches her, licking his lips. As she passes a table, she feels faint for a moment and leans on it to support herself.

Full-length shot of George standing face to camera behind the barrier. He has clasped one hand to his forehead and is shaking his head in an attempt to sober up.

Nogaro and Nellie seen by George: they appear hazy.

Nellie sets off again. Nogaro in the foreground at his table, Nellie walking slowly to the door. Nogaro looks in the owner's direction, frowning. He imperiously signals to him to be quiet.

Just as Nellie reaches the doorway, Nogaro stands up and shouts.

NOGARO: Nellie!

Come here, my little Nellie.

She turns round and looks at him.

She takes a few steps forward. He goes towards her, puts an arm around her shoulders and brings her back to his table.

Now, what's wrong, little Nellie?

Nellie falls back into an armchair and remains silent for a moment, staring straight ahead.

NELLIE: I haven't a penny to my name. I don't even know where I'm going to sleep tonight. I've been wandering round the town for two hours and . . . Oh, it's horrendous. There's death on the streets.

A pause. Nogaro strokes her hair and neck.

(*In a stubborn voice*): I don't mind dying. But not here!

Nogaro moves closer.

NOGARO: But you must come back to us, little Nellie.

Nellie nods in the direction of the (unseen) club owner.

NELLIE: He won't have it.

NOGARO: Who won't—Mercutio? But he's very nice, Mercutio. He does everything I want. Don't worry, little one, I'll fix it.

The owner, indignant and about to protest.

The owner, Nellie, her head bowed, and Nogaro leaning over Nellie. Above Nellie's head, he makes lordly gestures at the owner.

George takes a few steps towards the partition and falls back on to a chair with a vague expression in his eyes.

Nogaro with Nellie, face to camera, shot full-length, sitting at the table.

One thing, though, you'll have to be nice to me, Nellie. Very, very nice.

Nellie, overcome, speaks through clenched teeth.

NELLIE: As you like. I've got to live, after all.

Nogaro rubs his hands.

NOGARO (*to the unseen proprietor*): Well, that's arranged. Mercutio, you'll keep her on. She'll be as pliable and docile as a kitten.

A pause. He turns to Nellie.

                    Now, my dear, why are you looking so glum? In three months' time, you'll have enough money to go back to Europe.

On Nellie alone.

                    NELLIE (*as if to herself*): It's not *me* who'll be going back to Europe.

                    NOGARO: Who is it, then?

                    NELLIE: Someone else. Not me. *I*'m at an end. It's over. I'll never be able to pick myself up. I didn't think I could fall so low.

On Nogaro. He puts his arms round Nellie's shoulders and pulls her to him.

                    NOGARO: Well, no one could say you were a bundle of laughs. But you're well put together and you know how life is. You're nice. I like my women *very* nice.

She lets him tip her head over on to her shoulder.

                    You're nice, eh? Eh? You don't like me. I turn your stomach, but you're nice, eh?

He kisses her on the mouth and she offers no resistance.

George: face to camera, seated, a haziness in his eyes. All of a sudden, he sees

Nogaro kiss Nellie and his eyes flare with anger. He jumps up, more sober now.

George from behind, pushing through the little door into the European bar. He is moving quickly. He goes up to Nellie and Nogaro.

George, Nellie and Nogaro. Nellie pulls away smartly and stands up. She casts a furious glance at George. Nogaro is dumbfounded. He looks uncomprehendingly at the two of them.

GEORGE (*to Nellie*): Whore!

NELLIE (*harshly*): You can go and mind your own business! Go do the bear dance!

GEORGE: You've fallen even lower than me.

NELLIE: Well, you're happy, then. We're quits.

George takes her by the arm.

GEORGE: That's enough. You're coming with me.

Nogaro stands up and takes his riding whip from the table.

Nogaro and George, face to face, in profile.

He raises his whip to hit George in the face. George turns around and looks at him in astonishment, then grabs the

NOGARO: What's all this now, George? You're not very nice today. Come on, now, apologize to Miss Dixmier for disturbing us like this. Afterwards, you'll leave us alone, now, won't you?

whip from him and delivers a hefty punch to his face. Nogaro crumples to the ground. We hear a Homeric laugh.

Shot of the club owner bent double with laughter. He has tears in his eyes and is slapping his thighs.

OWNER: What about that, then, Nogaro? He's really sorted you out!

George and Nellie. George turns to Nellie, paying no attention now to Nogaro.

GEORGE: Get your things and follow me.

Rikko in a corner of the bar. He darts towards George.

George and Rikko. George gives Rikko such a look that Rikko steps back and directs all his attention to picking up the dazed Nogaro.

Nellie looks George proudly in the eye.

(*To Nellie*): Come on!

NELLIE: Hey, what's got into you? D'you think I'm afraid of you? Do you think I owe you something, perhaps? Well, you've got another think coming. Go on, I'll follow.

They make to leave. George has kept hold of the whip. At the door, two natives who stare at them.

GEORGE (*in cold, threatening tones*): Let us through, boys.

The Malays step aside. George and Nellie exit.

Shot of the club owner, still bent double with laughter.

*   *

The road. The Malays leaving (carts, wheelbarrows, entire families—all shot from behind). The Malays are moving slowly. A silent George and Nellie walk briskly, skipping between the carts. George takes large strides.

Nellie and George, face to camera, shot from the waist up. George, his face expressionless, his brows knit, walks a little way ahead of Nellie. We can see she is having difficulty keeping up, which adds to her fury.

NELLIE: Where are we going?

GEORGE: To my place.

Nellie and George in profile, walking between the natives.

An office in a barracks. An army major, face to camera, sitting at a desk and telephoning. Two lieutenants standing in front of him, shot from behind, full-length. We can see the major between the two lieutenants.

MAJOR: Very well, General. (*He hangs up.*) Lieutenants, you will take with you two teams of a hundred men and 15 lorries each. The first team will mount a roadblock on the Santareya road at the Sartha Rock. You'll turn back to Ottawee all the natives that try to pass. The second team will round up all the natives still in Shantytown and the surrounding area. You'll load them on to lorries and take them to the hospital, where they'll be vaccinated.

George and Nellie (right profile) outside George's cabin. The dog facing them, in left profile. On seeing Nellie, he growls. She takes a step back. George sniggers. Nellie dashes a furious glance at him and advances on the dog, which retreats growling. She opens the door and goes in. George goes in behind her.

The interior of the cabin. Nellie in the middle of the cabin, face to camera. George opposite her, a little to the left, in right profile, the riding whip in his hand. In the background, the barrel and the back of the cabin. A pause. Nellie looks George up and down.

The Malayan funeral chant dimly discernable in the background.

NELLIE: Well, what do you have to say to me?

GEORGE (*with clenched fists*): I shan't let you knock about with Nogaro.

George is so overcome with anger that he finds it difficult to speak. Nellie is as furious as he is, but hers is a cold rage.

NELLIE (*ironically*) You won't? And how are you going to stop me?

GEORGE: I shan't let you knock about with him.

NELLIE: Well, who's asking you for anything anyway? *Why* are you bothering about me?

GEORGE: You saw me dance the other day. You were there, all clean, elegant and carefree. And I was dancing like an animal. I want to wipe that away.

NELLIE: You'll never wipe it away.

On George.

GEORGE (*violently*): I shall. I'll destroy that image at the back of that wretched smug little mind of yours. You were looking down on me, eh? You were thinking, 'How can anyone fall so low? What a piece of trash, what a wreck of a man.' Ah! I'll save you! I'll save you from them and from yourself! And when you remember the wreck of a man dancing beneath the whip, then you'll have to say to yourself, 'It's that wreck who saved me from ending up in the gutter.' After that, if you can still despise me with-

With hatred in his voice.

George and Nellie.

On George, from the waist up.

Three buses filled with soldiers and three empty buses stop on the road outside Shantytown. We see the soldiers jump out and run off (in the distance, face to camera) towards Shantytown.

In Shantytown. Panic among the natives, who are trying to escape. The soldiers appear, enter the huts, bring the natives out, whining, and line them up.

The last huts at Shantytown. In the background, George's cabin (150 yards away). The soldiers go towards it.

In George's cabin. Nellie and George.

out despising yourself, then you'll be very lucky.

NELLIE (*hard-faced*): Charming. Perhaps you're expecting gratitude?

GEORGE: I don't give a damn for your gratitude. You can hate me if you want. (*Loudly*) But you won't despise me!

Squeals from the natives.

The NCOs are heard issuing orders.

NELLIE (*scornfully*): Stop me ending up in the gutter? You stupid bugger! Are *you* going to find me work? You've really screwed things up, you idiot. I know Nogaro's disgusting. But I can fall even lower. Do you know what's

On Nellie.

George and Nellie. George strikes her violently on the shoulders and arms with the riding whip.

The door in the background. George and Nellie in profile, shot from the back of the cabin. The door opens suddenly. George lets go of Nellie and soldiers come into the room. A lieutenant, a sergeant and two men. Nellie looks at George and sniggers.

left to me after what you did? The street.

GEORGE: I'll give you money.

NELLIE: You don't have any.

GEORGE: I'll get some.

NELLIE: Yes, from passers-by's pockets. I'd rather chuck myself in the river than take your money.

GEORGE: You'd rather sleep with Nogaro, wouldn't you?

NELLIE: I'd rather sleep with anybody.

GEORGE (*hitting her*): Slut! That's the kind of girl you are, is it? But I won't let you. I'll prevent you from knocking around with Nogaro.

Furious barking and the sounds of voices, as he hits her.

LIEUTENANT: What were you doing to this woman?

George doesn't reply.

Nelllie casts a triumphant glance at George. She turns round to the lieutenant, takes her time and says:

LIEUTENANT: Do you wish to press assault charges, miss?

The lieutenant hesitates. He looks at George and Nellie, then:

NELLIE: No, no. It was an argument . . . a lively one.

LIEUTENANT (*to George*): All right. It's none of my business. You're lucky. Come on, out! Off for your jabs.

GEORGE (*almost begging*): I'll go later. Leave me. This very evening, I promise.

LIEUTENANT (*to soldiers*): Take him.

The soldiers grab George, who struggles. Nellie is still laughing.

GEORGE: I'm . . . I'm European. You don't have the right to treat me like a native.

George, from behind, held up by the natives.[4] The lieutenant shot face to camera. The lieutenant hesitates, with the sergeant behind him.

LIEUTENANT (*hesitating*): That's the first time you've acknowledged your race.

The lieutenant and the sergeant.

SERGEANT: Race means nothing, Lieutenant. He lives like the natives. He's always with them. He's got to be full of lice.

On George, face to camera.

George and the soldiers, with the lieutenant in profile.

The soldiers push George towards the door.

Nellie at the back of the hut, sniggering.

GEORGE: Look, I swear I'll go this evening.

LIEUTENANT: Come on! Let's not mess about here. Get him on the lorry!

NELLIE: So, George, you'll sort things out for me now, will you? Stop me ending up in the gutter.

George and the soldiers. The soldiers push him through the doorway (shot from behind). He turns round.

These last words spoken when he is already outside.

GEORGE (*despairingly*): Stay here, Nellie. Stay! I'll get money, I swear. Wait for me, stay!

Nellie and the lieutenant (shot full-length, from the entrance to the cabin, Nellie face on and the lieutenant in three-quarter view). A pause. Nellie laughs. The lieutenant seems embarrassed.

LIEUTENANT: We have some buses here. Would you like to go back to town on one?

Nellie hesitates.

NELLIE: No . . . no thanks. I'll walk back.

Dissolve.

*   *

At the hospital. A large bare ward. At the very back, at a rectangular table, Thomas, Starrett and Sleep in white coats. They have the vaccination instruments in front of them. Nurses, male and female, are coming and going. To the right of the table, in the foreground, stands a crowd of frightened natives. Two nurses grab the natives one by one and virtually carry them to the doctors. The natives scream, whine and kick as they are dragged over.

View of a stout Malayan woman who is being taken over to the doctors. She is speaking shrilly and volubly in Malayan. The camera follows her. Thomas comes over to her.

DR THOMAS: Now, now, there's nothing to be afraid of.

Her dress is parted a little and she is given an injection in the back.

The Malayan woman talks more and more quickly.

Sleep hands her her vaccination certificate. The woman is dazed for a moment, then runs off screaming.

George in among the natives. Shot full-length, face to camera. Three Malays around him, the others less distinct to

GEORGE: There's money to be made. Lots of money.

the right and left and behind him, against the wall.

The Malay turns to his neighbour on the left and explains the scheme to him in Malayan with animated gestures.

The camera moves slowly along the crowd. We can see the news is being passed down the line.

The camera pulls back. We can see that what was at first a frightened herd has turned into a noisy, lively crowd as a result of George's proposition. At the back, the nurses are dragging along a Malay who is kicking and screaming.

Dissolve.

It's George's turn. He's at the front of the queue now, near the table. Two nurses come to fetch him. He follows them without needing to be dragged.

FIRST MALAY: But if I sell my card, won't they vaccinate me twice?

GEORGE: Twice, three times if you like. And each time we'll buy your certificate. Tell your pals. All those who want in just have to go to the fairground behind the Shadow Theatre as they come out. I'll come and meet you there.

The camera follows them. George, full-length in profile in front of the table. Dr Thomas, behind George, face to camera, leaning over his syringe. Sleep face to camera, sitting behind the table.

George doesn't reply. Dr Thomas looks up and stares at him. He is surprised at first, then indignant and compassionate.

DR THOMAS (*without looking at him*): That's good. You're not afraid then?

Aren't you George Astor?

GEORGE: What if I am?

DR THOMAS: What are you doing among the natives?

GEORGE: I was dragged here.

DR THOMAS: How has it come to this, George? How did you get like this?

GEORGE: That's my business.

Dr Thomas hesitates. On Thomas. He toys somewhat nervously with the syringe (shot from waist up).

DR THOMAS: Listen, George. I'm going to make you an offer. It's above my pay-grade, but I'll do it all the same.

A pause.

DR THOMAS: There's only four of us doctors for the whole town. That's not enough. Help us. Your place is by our side.

George and Thomas.

GEORGE (*sniggering*): I was struck off six years ago.

DR THOMAS: George, I know the Governor. If you want, I'm sure we could sort that out.

GEORGE: Do you know why I was struck off?

DR THOMAS: Yes. Well, in fact I do . . .

George's face has stiffened. He doesn't reply.

(*Insistently*): There are thousands of lives to be saved.

GEORGE (*averting his eyes and speaking between clenched teeth*): I don't give a damn.

Thomas reacts with a start and regards him attentively.

DR THOMAS: Well, as you will, George. As you will.

George turns round, rips off his jacket and silently presents his bare back for the injection.

Nellie shot full-length, face to camera, in the doorway of the hut. In the foreground, the dog growling. Nellie looks at the dog, then suddenly smiles at it. She bends down a little and calls to it.

NELLIE: Hey, come over here! Come, come.

The dog growls for a moment, then slowly comes over and allows itself to be stroked. Nellie standing outside the hut with the dog beside her.

The entrance to the 'Mount Everest'. The owner is smoking a cigar in the doorway (shot full-length, face to camera).

George in the street leading to the 'Mount Everest'. Walking, in profile.

The club owner in the doorway and George.

OWNER: Oh, it's you. Well, you've got some nerve.

George laughs.

GEORGE: How's Nogaro?

OWNER: So-so. What the hell brings you here?

GEORGE: The scam we talked about this morning—are you still up for it?

OWNER: That depends.

GEORGE: I've got 35 Malays waiting to sell me their cards.

OWNER (*eagerly*): Where?

GEORGE: What will you pay per card?

OWNER: Two dollars each.

GEORGE: Make it three.

OWNER: Three then, as it's you.

GEORGE: And my commission?'

OWNER: Five per cent.

GEORGE: Six.

OWNER (*grimaces, but nods agreement*): OK, six.

GEORGE: Come with me.

The owner wants to set off, but George stops him.

Hold on a minute. Is Nellie here?

OWNER: God, no!

George pushes him away, cranes his head over his shoulder and looks into the bar.

GEORGE: She hasn't been back then?

OWNER: No, and I'm telling you it's just as well she hasn't.

George, face to camera, alongside the owner. He looks reassured and is almost smiling.

Dissolve.

GEORGE: Phew.

*

*

George back at his cabin. He whistles for the dog, which doesn't respond, and opens the door.

George inside, standing by the door, face to camera. He is surprised.

Shot of Nellie sitting in the rocking chair. She is stroking the dog, which has its head on her lap.

George goes up to Nellie.

George and Nellie (from the waist up).

GEORGE (*showing no concern*): Oh, you're still here.

NELLIE (*harshly*): Where do you suppose I could go?

GEORGE: You can go back to the Victoria Hotel. I've paid your bill and a fortnight in advance . . . Here's some money for you.

He takes two banknotes out of his pocket.

NELLIE: Where did you steal that from?

GEORGE: I didn't steal it, I earned it.

On Nellie. She is looking at the money.

NELLIE: You did that for me?

On George.

GEORGE: No need for sentiment. You know very well why I did it.

Nellie and George. At George's last words, her face has clouded over. She turns the banknotes over and over in her hands.

NELLIE: You earned that in four hours? That's a bit of a surprise.

With a kind of naivety.

GEORGE: It's a scam.

NELLIE: What scam?

GEORGE: Mercutio's buying up the poor Malays' vaccination certificates to sell them to those who don't want vaccinating.

NELLIE: And you?

GEORGE: I'm the go-between.

On Nellie. She begins to laugh bitterly.

NELLIE: Bah! I was being too naive. How would you have earned that money honestly? No point asking the impossible.

GEORGE: OK, it's an illegal scheme. I can understand you're disgusted. Whereas prostitution, that . . . that's within the bounds of the law, so no problem there.

NELLIE: If I went on the streets, I'd not be harming anyone but myself.

GEORGE: I'm not harming anyone.

NELLIE: Are you totally unaware of what you're doing? I know they've only got a little vaccine, the nurse told me. To make four or five dollars, you're exposing half the population to typhus.

Shot, from the waist up and in profile, of Nellie and George squaring up to each other.

And that's not all. These poor sods who are selling their cards are going to get three or four injections to earn a few pennies. They're risking their lives.

GEORGE: It's of their own free will.

NELLIE: But you should know you don't have any *free will* when you're dying of hunger.

GEORGE: Oh, well, I couldn't care less. If you don't want the money, give it back to me. I won't have any trouble spending it.

NELLIE: Of course you won't. So long as there's whisky in the bars, you won't have any trouble. There's your money.

She throws the crumpled notes in George's face. They fall to the floor.

A silence. George casts a mean glance at her.

GEORGE: Right. Goodbye, then. Old Ma Flossie's expecting you at the Victoria Hotel.

NELLIE: I'm not going to the Victoria Hotel. It's this money you used to pay for my room, isn't it?

A pause.

On Nellie. She still looks severe, but she averts her eyes a little as she speaks.

NELLIE: You've got me into a mess. You can get me out of it. I'm staying here.

On George, full-length.

GEORGE (*curtly*): That's your problem. The cabin's yours. I'll sleep outside.

He turns around.

George, shot from behind, by the door. He turns around, whistles for the dog, which comes to him, opens the door and goes out, followed by the dog.

Evening is falling. Outside the doors of the hospital. Mercutio and Rikko in . . . [5]

Night. George's cabin by moonlight. George, wrapped in a blanket and lying outside the cabin door. His dog is sleeping alongside him. George can't sleep. He turns over, then gets up, goes over to the door and listens.

The interior of the cabin. Nellie lying on the mat. She cannot sleep and sits up on it. Moonlight streams in through a wide-open window and we can see her distinctly. She hears the noise, looks towards the door, then quickly lies down again and closes her eyes.

Sound of a door creaking.

Shot of the door opening slowly. George comes in on tiptoe and closes the door behind him.

George beside Nellie's bed. He looks at her, then leans over her. He takes the blanket and lays it over Nellie with a kind of affection. Then he turns around and makes to leave. At that point, Nellie sits up and looks at him.

Every trace of affection disappears from George's face, giving way to a kind of spiteful discomfiture. He doesn't want to be caught with his guard down. He hesitates, assumes his spineless, cynical attitude once more and drops down to sit beside her.

She looks at him, more in disappointment than fear.

He draws her towards him, but without violence. She is leaning against him. There is a brief moment of silent, stifling sensuality between them, without

NELLIE (*with no harshness in her voice*): What are you doing here?

GEORGE: I thought to myself—she's not used to sleeping alone. She needs a little pal to keep her warm.

I thought—either she wants to or she doesn't. If she wants to, she won't need any sweet-talking. Two old trollops like us can always come to some arrangement.

either dropping their guard. And then Nellie pulls away—without difficulty.

On Nellie.

NELLIE: That was the only decent thing you had left—that a woman could sleep safely at your place. At least, I thought so. If I was wrong, what have you got?

George stares at her, uncertain, embarrassed and moved by what she has just said.

GEORGE: Did you think that of me?

NELLIE: Think what?

GEORGE: That a woman could sleep in peace at my place.

On Nellie.

On George. He has recovered his ironic tone.

NELLIE (*curtly*): Yes. I did.

GEORGE (*ironically*): You'll have to excuse me. You're the first person to find anything decent in me for seven years.

NELLIE (*severely*): It didn't take you long to dispel my illusions.

On Nellie and George.

A silence. George tries to find a way out. He sees the banknotes on the floor.

GEORGE: Ah, and then I came in to pick up the money too. You still don't want it?

Nellie shakes her head.

He turns away and picks them up.

He gets up, pockets the notes, gives Nellie a little wave, turns around and goes to the door.

The door closing behind him.

Nellie sitting on the mat, supporting herself on her two hands pressed flat to the floor. She stares towards the door.

Dissolve.

*

At the 'Mount Everest' bar in the morning. The chairs are on the tables and Rikko is washing the floor. Mercutio, his head bandaged, looking half-asleep, is smoking a cigar. Nogaro, with a black eye, is playing patience.

The entrance to the 'Mount Everest' seen from the interior. George comes in.

Right. Well, no point hoarding the stuff, is there?

NELLIE: What are you going to do with it?

GEORGE: What do you think I'm going to do? I'm going to drink to your health.

*

Nogaro and the club owner see George come in and exchange a glance.

Nogaro and Mercutio, and George moving towards them. He throws the money on the table. The banknotes on top of the cards.

GEORGE: Here's your money. I'm out of this. I used the cash that's missing to pay for Nellie Dixmier a room at the 'Victoria Hotel'. She doesn't want it, so you can have it.

Mercutio and Nogaro exchange glances. Nogaro looks at George with a hatred he has difficulty concealing beneath an affectionate exterior.

NOGARO: You're no longer with us on this, George? That's not nice. Didn't it occur to you that you could be putting us in an awkward position?

GEORGE: You'll find some other scheme. I'm not going to lose any sleep over you.

George and Nogaro. Nogaro smiles.

NOGARO: You're right, George. You're right not to lose any sleep over us. Because we were already wondering last night what might happen if you changed your mind. We thought, we wouldn't want you to feel bad on our account. So Mercutio did a deal directly with the natives.

George stares at them, dumbfounded.

GEORGE: Bastards!

Nogaro pushes the banknotes away and goes on with his patience.

NOGARO: You know, young George, in business, it's always best to cut out the middle man . . . And it turns out we were right, since you're leaving us in the lurch.

George turns towards Mercutio.

GEORGE: Listen, Mercutio, I've given this some thought. You *can't* go on. It's filthier than murder. Perhaps you don't know that there isn't enough vaccine for everyone.

MERCUTIO: What of it?

GEORGE: Then people are going to die from your little scheme.

MERCUTIO: Bah! only Malays . . .

GEORGE: Don't you want to stop it, while there's still time?

Mercutio says nothing, but takes a huge puff on his cigar and blows the smoke out voluptuously down his nose. Nogaro, absorbed in turning over the cards in his game of patience, says nothing.

The owner is now standing. Rikko comes over. George in profile, the owner face to camera.

Right, then I'll stop you going on with it. I'm telling you.

OWNER: *You'll* stop us? *You'll* stop us?

Nogaro has not got up. He raises his hand.

NOGARO (*in wheedling tones*): Listen, young George. It's wrong of you to talk like that. We like you a lot, you know. And violence isn't really our game. If you make trouble for us, you'll hurt us, hurt us a lot, and that's all there is to it. Only we have some pals who are a bit hot-headed, a bit quick to take offence. They're just kids, eh! Only, if they decided some punishment was in order, there's a danger we couldn't stop them.

GEORGE: Is that it? Well, what I'm telling you is that one way or another I'll see to it that these dealings of yours come to an end. After that, you can do what you want.

He turns on his heels.

Nogaro still seated, the owner standing. Both in the foreground, seen from behind. The door in the background. We see George exit. A short silence.

NOGARO: Rikko, be so kind as to take a little walk behind our friend there. You can tell us what he's up to.

*

*

The police inspector in his office. A bare room with whitewashed walls. A barred window giving on to a tropical garden seen from the first floor. A rectangular black wooden table, its left side leaning against the wall by the window. The inspector in profile at the table. Diagonal shot of inspector, window and table.

A police officer in the foreground, on the other side of the table, facing the inspector.

INSPECTOR: You can show him in now.

The officer goes out. The inspector pulls a bottle of whisky out of a little low cupboard to his left and puts it on the table.

Enter George. He goes up to the table and remains standing. He is shot full-length, in the foreground, with only the outline of his cheek visible.

Hello, George.

George is silent. He remains at the table, his arms dangling.

I think I know why you're here. You heard a nice little story this morning and you thought, 'I know the inspector. He likes stories. I'll go and tell him it.' Is that it?

The inspector taps lighly on the bottle with a ruler.

George hesitates.

His face in close-up. He appears hesitant and pained.

George and the inspector, face to camera.

George bows and leaves.

Inspector, face to camera, bewildered.

The hospital, vaccination ward. Starrett at the table, Thomas standing, and a Malay.

GEORGE: Might be.

INSPECTOR: Do you see this bottle? Well, if your story makes me laugh, it's yours.

Go on, then. Oh, by the way, for that story about the bales of rice . . . thank you! The chap tried to skedaddle, but we found him, because there's an army road block now at the Sartha Rock. He ran smack into it and they brought him back to us. He's doing two years.

GEORGE: Two years!

INSPECTOR: I'm listening.

GEORGE (*suddenly*): I just came to tell you not to count on me any longer. My informing days are over. Goodbye, Inspector.

DR THOMAS: I've a feeling I've seen that

The Malay gives a hearty laugh and shakes his head.

The Malay nods, still laughing.

The Malay presents his back. Dr Thomas takes the syringe.

George appears in the doorway.

Dr Thomas looks up and George comes over to him. George, shot from behind, moving from left to right towards Dr Thomas, who is on the right. On the far right, the crowd of Malays.

George gets to Thomas and stands facing him, in profile.

The native, in profile, turned towards the left. Dr Thomas, to the right of the native, turned to the right. George, to the right of Dr Thomas and turned towards him.

face before. Have you ever been vaccinated?

Do you swear you haven't?

You know it could kill you? Right, let's see your back.

GEORGE: Stop a moment, please.

Half of these have already been vaccinated.

DR THOMAS: I thought as much. But how am I going to recognize them?

GEORGE: I know them all. I'll recognize the ones who were here yesterday. First, get this one out of here.

DR THOMAS (*to some male nurses*): Get this chap out of here.

Two nurses take hold of the Malay and drag him to the door, kicking him up the backside.

Dr Thomas turns to the Malays.

GEORGE: Right, now get the others to parade in front of me.

DR THOMAS (*to the Malays*): Come on. Over here. Two by two.

The Malays file past. George takes one out by the arm, then another and another. As he pulls them out of the ranks, the nurses kick them out of the room. The Malays taken out of the line run off shouting. The doctors begin to laugh and the Malays too. George himself smiles.

GEORGE: Vaccinated, vaccinated. That one too. And that one.

Shot of Rikko on tiptoe, looking in through a window. We see the scene of the expulsion through the pane that isn't hidden by his head. Rikko moves away from the window pane and goes on his way.

George and Dr Thomas.

Is this the whole of the morning batch?

DR THOMAS: Yes.

GEORGE: All right. I'll be back at two o'clock to see the others.

Rikko at the 'Mount Everest' standing in front of Nogaro and the club owner, who are sitting at a table. At the back and to the left, five shady-looking muscular types are drinking at another table.

RIKKO: He grabbed them by the arm and pulled them out of the line.

NOGARO: Right! Right! Right!

Nogaro picks up the cards from his game of patience, forms them into a single pack, which he lays on the table, and walks over slowly to the gangsters' table, followed by the owner.

The gangsters (who will be described below), Nogaro and the owner.

He sits down on a chair.

We've got some work for you, boys.

There's a fellow who's not behaved nicely to us . . .

The vaccination ward. Full-length shot, in profile, of George and Dr Thomas, standing facing each other a little apart.

DR THOMAS: You can see you should be helping us.

George does not reply.

You've only got to say the word, George.

George takes him by the shoulders.

GEORGE: Thomas, I'm never coming back here.

DR THOMAS: You're not? Then it's

On George.

because you don't want to. We're ready to take you back.

GEORGE: What about me? Do you think I'm ready to take myself back. The prodigal son, eh? You welcome him with open arms, wipe the slate clean and start over again? But what can you wipe clean? How stupidly vain you are, you decent people? Just because I'm back among you and you're shaking my hand, while keeping a discreet eye on me, you think that'll be enough to make me feel rehabilitated. I don't give a damn for rehabilitation, Thomas. I don't give a damn for the decent people. It's me I'm afraid of. I'm the only one who's entitled to rehabilitate and forgive myself. And I can't. I hate myself. I'm a doomed man and I like it that way.

On Thomas.

DR THOMAS: There aren't any doomed men. There are men who strive, out of pride, to doom themselves. You're too proud, George.

George holds out his hands.

GEORGE: Look at my hands. They're shaking because I'm awash with alcohol. My memory's gone, I'm half gaga.

The floating bottle. We hear George's voice and the bottle continues to float.

Don't you think that's enough to make me a doomed man? It was my decision, Thomas, my decision. Do you know what I've been doing for six years? I've been paying. I tied a stone round my neck, to sink me to the bottom. And now I'm at the bottom and I shan't come up again. (*He laughs*) Ha, what a doctor I'd be . . .

On George, from the waist up. He goes on:

And I'm telling you, I shan't be around for much longer. There are some people out to get me. And they will. So, leave me alone.

George and Dr Thomas, from the waist up.

Dr Thomas extends a hand, but George doesn't take it.

DR THOMAS: As you wish.

GEORGE: No, no. No fuss. Stay where you are. You don't want to be mixing with people like me. Better to give me a quid so I can go and have a drink.

Dr Thomas hesitates, then pulls out a banknote.

George turns on his heels and leaves.

Thanks.

*

*

George in the street. Rikko follows him. He goes into a bar and sits down at a table.

Dissolve.

Outside the bar. Rikko is walking in front and the five gangsters behind, in groups of two and three. Rikko is shot from behind and the gangsters in profile (from left to right). As he passes the bar, Rikko turns around and gives the gangsters a nod and a wink. He then walks on paying no heed to them. The gangsters casually enter the bar.

Interior of the bar. The gangsters come in. They are: 1) an enormous brute, unshaven and wearing a trilby with a feather in it, a white suit that is too tight for him and an open-necked shirt with no tie; 2) a fiercely handsome little man—too much the pretty boy—with fair, curly hair. He is very short, dressed up to the nines, wearing a bow-tie; when he walks, he virtually skips along; 3) a long, thin melancholic type; 4) a hefty, neatly dressed, dark-haired handsome man of Italian appearance with a nasty look about him; 5) a stout, but sturdy

GEORGE: A bottle of whisky.

red-headed bull-necked man, with a stiff little moustache and waddling gait.

They look around for George and find him at the back of the room. They go over unhurriedly, the little curly-haired man arm in arm with the big brute.

The gangsters from behind, moving towards George. George in the far background sees them and realizes what is happening. He is lighting a cigarette. He drops the lit match which falls to the floor and goes out.

George's table. The five gangsters standing in a semi-circle around the table, shot full-length from behind. George, face on, on the other side of the table, is seen between the curly-haired little man and the tall thin one.

THE TALL HEFTY MAN: How's tricks?

GEORGE: Fine, thanks. Sit yourselves down.

CURLY LITTLE MAN: We're not disturbing you?

GEORGE: No, you don't know how good it is to see you.

The owner comes over.

OWNER: What can I get you?

THE ITALIAN: Do you have a kitchen?

OWNER: Er, yes.

THE ITALIAN: Well, go see if we're in there. We need to have a serious chat with your pal here. Understood?

On the owner.

Wide-eyed with surprise, the owner retreats out of the shot.

Silence.

GEORGE: You're not very talkative.

No answer. Two of the five (the Italian and the tall melancholic) get up and come and stand to George's right and left. The others remain seated. George pours himself a glass of whisky.

The same, seen in profile from the right. Both the gangsters and George seem under some sort of spell. They look at each other and we don't know whether George is fascinated by the gangsters or they by him.

On the curly-haired little man, face to camera. He seems gentle but stubborn. He yawns noisily.

STOUT RED-HEADED MAN: Are you sleepy, Babyface?

BABYFACE: No, I always yawn before we start. It passes off afterwards.

On George. He is drinking.

GEORGE: What are you waiting for?'

THE ITALIAN: Hey, don't tell me you're in a bigger hurry than we are?

They lean over to George, keeping their eyes on him constantly.

They turn around.

The door to the bar. The inspector has just entered. He smiles as he surveys the scene. The Italian gets up immediately.

TALL MELANCHOLIC: Hold it, boys!

He shakes his hand.

THE ITALIAN: So, bye then, George. We'll see each other soon, eh?

GEORGE: Of course we will. Of course.

BABYFACE: Goodbye, pal.

He shakes his hand.

Close-up on George's hand, successively shaking the hands of the other three (hands with rings—large signet rings, etc.). The gangsters face to camera by the entrance. They leave in the order in which they entered, with a slow, rolling gait. The inspector, from behind, on the right.

(*As he passes by*): Hello, Inspector.

INSPECTOR: Hello.

The inspector goes over to George's table and sits down. The inspector on the left in profile. George face to camera.

You keep some strange company.

GEORGE: They're some pals of mine.

INSPECTOR: I've just come from the hospital. I've seen Dr Thomas.

GEORGE (*polite and indifferent*): Oh?

INSPECTOR: He likes you, Dr Thomas. He spoke highly of you. (*Pause*) Say, you don't know who's been doing a trade in vaccination cards, do you?

George shakes his head.

Because I was just thinking, perhaps that's what George came to tell me earlier . . .

George remains silent.

At any rate, if your little pals were causing you trouble, we could help you, couldn't we? We owe you that much, at least.

George shrugs his shoulders.

GEORGE: I don't need anyone's help.

INSPECTOR: Well, that's your business. Oh, try and keep something on you, won't you? A card or your address, so that we can identify you. You'll save us some time with the investigation. When they've worked a guy over properly, it can be a bit hard to recognize him.

GEORGE: I'm not particularly concerned about being recognized.

He pours himself a glass of whisky and drinks it.

*

*

Nellie in George's cabin. She has made herself a broom out of a branch and some leaves and is sweeping away the cobwebs. She seems animated and almost joyful.

She gets up on a chair. Shot of a corner of the ceiling with an enormous spider's web. The spider is in the middle.

Nellie in profile, shot from the waist up, destroying the cobweb with the broom. The spider gets away. Nellie chases it into the back left-hand corner of the cabin. The spider slips under a little cupboard.

Nellie by the cupboard, puzzled. She pulls out the top drawer. It is empty. She pulls out the bottom drawer and brings out a parcel messily wrapped in newspaper.

Nellie at the table. Nellie, shot head and shoulders and in profile, unwraps the parcel. She brings out a white uniform with epaulettes, like the one George is wearing in the photograph.

The cabin door opens (face on to the camera). Nellie hastily puts the uniform back on the table and tries to reassemble the parcel.

The entrance to the cabin, shot from the interior. George comes in with the dog. George face to camera. He is carrying Nellie's two cases and the birdcage. He is unsteady on his feet.

George and Nellie, face to face in profile.

GEORGE: Here are your cases.

She makes to thank him, then realizes his eyes are glazed and he's unsteady on his feet.

NELLIE: You've been drinking.

GEORGE: So what? I told you I would. You didn't think I was going to take that money you threw in my face and chuck it in the bin, did you?

On Nellie. She looks at him incredulously.

NELLIE: Is it that money you've been drinking?

GEORGE: Yes, indeed!

Nellie comes over to him and looks him in the eye.

NELLIE: You're lying!

George sniggers. He hiccups.

You're lying. I'm getting to know you. You didn't touch it. You've given it back to Mercutio. And don't you think I understood your little game last night? What is it that's so rotten in you that you have to try to make yourself more despicable than you are? There you are, spineless, filthy and drunk, you lie to me and I . . .

On Nellie.

You make me feel so ashamed.

She gives a few nervous sobs.

She wipes her eyes and stops crying. George looks at her in astonishment. Then he turns away and looks at the table.

The uniform on the table, shot from above.

George and Nellie. George begins to laugh and points to the uniform.

GEORGE: So you've unearthed that thing. (*He laughs*) It's a laugh, eh? Have you seen the spots of rust on it?

NELLIE: I don't find it funny. You were a

naval doctor once and . . . look what's become of you.

*

*

The Santareya road outside Shantytown. Mercutio's five killers in the car. The little, fair-haired man is driving.

George and Nellie. Behind them, the table and the portrait. George turns around and points to the portrait.

GEORGE: So, you like me better like that?

NELLIE: I don't know. Why, oh why have you fallen so low?

GEORGE: I was a young fool. Just look at that. Just look at that vanity, that complacency. He thought he was a man because he'd passed some exams. Bastard! Bastard!

He takes the uniform.

He wore that thing. He kissed some hands. Do you realize: that there was me!

NELLIE: But what did you do?

GEORGE: Me, nothing. He's the one who did everything, him, the young

On George.

He becomes gloomy and distraught.

He bangs his fist on his chest.

On Nellie. She gives him an imperious stare.

George and Nellie.

On Nellie, dumbfounded.

On the road, the gangsters' car.

sod with the qualifications. I'm just paying for the breakages.

No, that's not true, Nellie. He's me. We're one and the same person. It was me: *I* did everything. Me here now. Me that I hate. Me, the same spineless, cowardly man as before.

NELLIE: That's enough, George. Cut the play-acting. Tell me what you did.

GEORGE: It would take too long, Nellie. I don't have the time. Because we're going to say our farewells.

NELLIE: You're . . . you're leaving?

GEORGE: I think I'm going to be taking a little journey. I'm waiting for some pals who are going to take me with them.

NELLIE (*downcast and very hard-faced*): Where are you going?

GEORGE: I don't know yet.

NELLIE: Is it the typhus that frightens you?

GEORGE: No.

NELLIE: What about me? Had you given any thought to what was to become of me?

Engine noise. The dog growls.

Nellie and George look at the dog in silence. George walks to the door.

The entrance, wide-open. George, from behind, standing in the doorway. He is silent for a moment, then turns round to Nellie.

GEORGE: Ask for Dr Thomas at the hospital. Tell him I asked him to look after you and to send you home as soon as it becomes possible.

On Nellie.

NELLIE (*hissing with anger*): Right. Very good. Have a good trip! You came into my life without so much as a by-your-leave, you ruined everything and now you're leaving again, with a satisfied conscience, passing me on to somebody else like a parcel. Have a good trip—a good trip! You really are as cowardly as they come.

George face to camera in the cabin doorway, shot from the exterior. He is looking at the road.

On the road, in the distance, the five killers. The car stops. They get out and begin to walk up to George's cabin.

George turns around and goes back into the cabin.

George inside the cabin. He kneels down by the dog and ties it to the wall.

GEORGE (*as he is tying up the dog*): I've done what I was trying to, Nellie. I've wiped out of your mind the awful image you had of me. I challenge you now to think of me as that drunken brute dancing under the riding whip.

NELLIE: The image you're leaving me with isn't much better.

GEORGE: It's more complicated. At least that's something.

George gets up and, in the cabin doorway, turns around.

The dog and Nellie. The dog growls louder. Nellie goes to the doorway.

The five killers, face to camera, heading for the cabin.

Nellie and George face to camera, full-length, in the doorway, shot from the exterior.

NELLIE: Who are these people?

GEORGE: They're my pals. They've come for me.

NELLIE: Why did you tie the dog up?

GEORGE (*still looking towards the killers*): He'll be so sad to see me go: he might bite them.

NELLIE (*forcefully, anxious*): George, who are these people? I'm sure of one thing, they're not your friends.

The five gangsters, face on. Babyface and the Italian in front, the others behind.

On George.

On the gangsters, who come closer.

George and Nellie and the gangsters in profile, shot from the right.

He pulls out his revolver.

George turns round to Nellie.

GEORGE: Go back into the cabin. They won't hurt you. They're polite to ladies.

THE ITALIAN: It's us, George.

GEORGE: So I see.

THE ITALIAN: We were interrupted earlier. We didn't get to have a proper talk.

GEORGE: I was expecting you.

THE ITALIAN: Come on out.

NELLIE: Who are you? What do you want with him?

GEORGE (*softly*): Go away, Nellie. It's over. There are just a few, rather unpleasant formalities to be completed.

THE ITALIAN: Is that the chick who sang at the 'Mount Everest'?

NELLIE: What are you going to do to him? I shan't leave him.

GEORGE (*to the Italian*): Get one of your men to look after her. In the cabin. Four of you will be enough for what you have to do.

THE ITALIAN: Babyface, look after the little lady. And be polite.

Babyface comes towards Nellie and pushes her back inside the cabin.

NELLIE: Let go of me! Let go of me!

He pushes her. She scratches him. He grabs her wrists and pushes her inside. George turns around and shuts the door. Then he faces up to the gangsters and waits.

THE ITALIAN: So, George! You tried to shop the boss?

He punches him right in the face. George reels, but doesn't defend himself.

You went for a bit of a chat with the men in blue, eh?

Another punch. The four gangsters surround him and beat him up.

Nellie inside the cabin. She is fighting with the curly-haired man, who has his hands full. The dog barks and pulls on its chain. Nellie tries to get to the door, but he prevents her. Then she pretends to have calmed down, but, while he— without taking his eyes off her—is taking a breather and readjusting his collar, she rushes to the dog and tries to let it off its chain. Babyface tries to stop her, but the dog throws itself on him. He steps back and pulls out his revolver.

BABYFACE: If you untie that poor mutt, sweetie, it gets it right between the eyes.

Outside, George has fallen to his knees. His nose is bleeding, his mouth swollen and one eye is closed. The gangsters carry on hitting him.

Nellie has untied the dog, which hurls itself at Babyface. He jumps back and takes aim.

Outside, the gangsters are still hitting George. A shot is heard from inside the cabin. George suddenly straightens.

GEORGE: What's that . . . what is it?

He manages to stand up, but the big red-head punches him in the stomach. George goes down from his full height, landing flat on his face.

He whistles through his teeth. The cabin door opens. Babyface appears, looking in a sorry state.

THE ITALIAN: That's enough

He whistles.

THE ITALIAN: Was it you who fired?

BABYFACE: There was a dog. I shot it.

THE ITALIAN: Let's clear out.

Nellie appears in the doorway, breathless and reeling.

The five killers from behind, running. Nellie looks at George's body without moving.

Sound of the engine starting.

174

In the distance, the killers' car starts up. It turns round and disappears.

Nellie in the foreground, still motionless. George lifeless.

George stirs weakly and groans. Nellie looks at him, but does not move. George opens his eyes, drags himself to the wall of the cabin and manages to sit down, leaning against it. A pause. He spits and wipes the back of his hand across his mouth. Then he puts a finger into his mouth and feels his teeth.

He hasn't seen Nellie yet. He turns his head towards her and notices her.

GEORGE (*muttering to himself*): They've broken some teeth.

Oh, you're there, are you? I thought they'd shot you?

NELLIE: No, they shot the dog.

A pause.

GEORGE (*with difficulty*): I thought they wanted to bump me off. But I'm not the type for bumping off, I'm the type for beating up.

He tries to get up, but can't. He spits.

My head hurts.

He gives a wicked laugh, but stops quickly since his lips hurt.

I really got it there! And I was talking about a long trip. But I'm alive, I'm alive. Let's be glad about that. Is the dog dead?

NELLIE: Yes.

GEORGE: The bastards! Couldn't they have shot me? Or you?

He tries to get up. He gets to his knees and then he manages gradually to stand. He leans against the wall.

If they'd shot you, you wouldn't be there looking at me with those damned bright eyes of your. (*To himself*) I thought they were going to kill me . . . (*To Nellie, suddenly*) Go away! Why do you have to stand there like that, looking at me? Go away! You've won. I can't bear to see you any more.

Nellie makes a move towards him.

No. Not your pity. Don't come playing the nursemaid. Go away and take your memories with you.

NELLIE: I know. You're much too proud to accept care from a nurse. But if I tell you I love you, will you take my arm to go back into your cabin?

George turns his head painfully towards Nellie and stares at her.

George's face in close-up.

Dissolve.

*   *

Four days later, at the hospital. Thomas and Starrett in their office. Thomas is telephoning and Starrett writing. He has a nervous tic (he blinks from time to time and his right shoulder twitches as he does so).

DR THOMAS: Yes, right. Right away. (*To Starrett*) Lemonnier's younger daughter. A 13-year-old kid!

DR STARRETT: Typhus?

DR THOMAS: Yes, the first case among the Whites.

DR STARRETT (*nervous*): It's starting. And there'll be no stopping it. It'll see off the lot of us.

DR THOMAS (*softly*): Starrett, you have to go to the Lemonniers.

DR STARRETT: But I've been on the go for 48 hours solid.

DR THOMAS: I know. It's Sleep who should go, but he isn't here. I don't know what he's doing.

Starrett gives Thomas a hard stare, then stands up without a word, takes his hat from the desk and goes out.

The office door, from the inside. Starrett opens it and bumps into the director as he leaves. The director turns round before entering and watches Starrett go.

DIRECTOR: What's the matter with him?

The director closes the door and comes over to Thomas.

The director and Thomas, from the waist up, face to face, in profile.

Thomas winces.

Thomas shrugs his shoulders, indicating that he doesn't know. A pause. The director goes over to the window.

Through the window we see an overhead shot of cars driving off with mattresses and trunks on their roofs. On the

DR THOMAS: He's out on his feet. He worries me.

DIRECTOR: I've just been informed there are about 50 cases among the natives in the dock area. The hospital hasn't even a straw mattress left to put them on. We can't take them.

DR THOMAS: I know. A doctor will have to set up over there with nurses and treat them on the spot.

DIRECTOR: I'll send Starrett.

DR THOMAS: It'll be hard work. In the state he's in . . . I think I'd better go myself.

DIRECTOR: No, Thomas. You've got to stay here. You're indispensable to the running of the hospital. Sleep will go. Where is he?

pavement opposite, three shops with their steel shutters lowered. At a fourth, a man is turning a handle and the shutter is coming down quickly.

The sound of a door opening. They turn around.

DR THOMAS: It's panic out there.

The door, wide open. Starrett in the doorway.

He throws his hat on to the desk.

Silence.

DR STARRETT (*with a strange look about him*): The kid's done for . . .

Where's Sleep?

He is standing, face to camera, in the middle of the room. Increasing nervousness. Twitches.

Behind him, Sleep is framed in the open door. His tie is undone and he is unshaven, pale and very stiff. Starrett turns round suddenly and lets out a cry.

Sleep, comes forward with difficulty, very stiffly, into the middle of the room, to Starrett's side.

Sleep!

Sleep and Starrett, shot full-length and from behind. Thomas and the director face to camera.

Sleep staggers forward. Starrett moves away swiftly, watching him with a

DIRECTOR (*severely*): Sleep, you're late. Mountain's had to take over your rounds. In the present circumstances, falling down on the job is criminal.

hunted look and pressing himself against the wall. Thomas springs forward and manages to hold Sleep up.

SLEEP: I'm done for, Thomas. I've got typhus.

Starrett suddenly straightens, wide-eyed with fear. He makes for the door, advancing mechanically.

DIRECTOR: Starrett!

Starrett carries on walking as though he has not heard him.

Starrett, stay here! That's an order.

Starrett from behind. He crosses the threshold of the office and slams the door behind him.

Starrett bringing his car to a halt outside his home. He jumps out and runs into the building, which is a European-style block of six or seven storeys.

Starrett climbing the stairs. When he gets to the landing, he opens the door to his flat.

Two male nurses supporting Sleep come out of Dr Thomas's office.

DR THOMAS (*to the director*): We have to try something. Give him a call.

Thomas and the director. Face to camera, by the table.

DIRECTOR: Do you think he's gone home?

He picks up the telephone and dials a number.

To Thomas (covering the telephone with his hand).

Hello, hello—Starrett?

He's there. He's hung up.

Hello, hello, Starrett! Hello. Come on, old man, answer!

Starrett at home, the receiver to his ear. He has a hunted look. Beside him are two open cases and toilet items, clothes and underclothes ready to be piled into the cases.

The director telephoning.

Starrett! Don't do anything stupid. Think about this. It's just a moment's depression. Don't go and . . .

A gesture of annoyance.

He's hung up.

*

*

Nellie sitting on the ground, George lying on the mat. He is tossing around in his sleep. Silence. She looks at him and swats the flies away with her hand. He wakes up (his swollen face is covered in bandages, with sticking plasters at the corner of his lips and on his cheek). He looks at her through half-closed eyes, then gets up painfully.

GEORGE: Are you still there, Nellie. You shouldn't be. Why did you stay?

NELLIE (*curtly*): I told you the day before yesterday.

George takes her hand.

GEORGE: You're wrong to love me. It's demeaning for you. I'm a useless old bastard, you know that.

NELLIE (*affectionately*): You're a soul in torment, that's what you are. A walking bundle of wounded pride. And what pride! It's all extremes with you: it's either the heights or the depths. You didn't reach the top, so you make every effort to get everyone to despise you. That didn't work with me. I don't despise you George. I respect you, because you're the most demanding of men.

On George.

George listens to her extremely attentively, but when she has finished, his face darkens.

GEORGE: Who are you to respect me, poor old Nellie? I don't respect you. And you won't be the one to restore my pride.

On Nellie.

NELLIE (*wounded*): Do you even know where I started out from? What entitles you to condemn me? I could have let my pride sink me straight to the bottom too. I didn't let it. I tried to keep my head above water. There's nothing brilliant in that, I know, but it's not been very easy either. I've had to show some guts.

George shrugs his shoulders.

GEORGE: Maybe so. But I tell you we'd make a miserable couple. Can you imagine it? Each of us tending the wounds to the other's self-esteem . . . No way! We're too ugly. You can put up with one loser, you can forget them, but *two*? Two of them looking into each other's eyes, fussing over and consoling each other—it's enough to make you sick.

There's a knock at the door. Nellie jumps up suddenly. She is worried.

The door, shot from the interior.

Dr Thomas comes in. Face to camera, shot full-length. He is surprised to see Nellie there.

Thomas coming forward. Nellie and George. Thomas nods to Nellie, who nods in reply. He looks at George and lets slip an admiring whistle.

NELLIE: What's that?

GEORGE: This is nothing. Just some

friends who came round to give me a thrashing.

DR THOMAS: Doesn't look like they were amateurs.

GEORGE: They're a team of specialists.

DR THOMAS: Was it to do with this vaccination business?

GEORGE (*shrugging his shoulders*): That was part of it. And then I was a bit too chatty in a general sort of way.

While talking, George has got up with difficulty and gone over to the table. His white uniform is still on it. He leans back against the table and, with his hands behind his back, knocks it off the table to hide it from Thomas's view.

DR THOMAS: George, come and help us.

GEORGE: I've already told you no.

DR THOMAS: That was two days ago. One of us has caught the typhus since then and another one has legged it.

GEORGE: Hey, that reminds me of something. Was he a young bloke?

DR THOMAS: The one who's ill?

GEORGE: No, the other one.

DR THOMAS: Quite young.

GEORGE: Poor sod.

DR THOMAS: The other day, you refused to help us because it was too easy. Now it's not so easy any more. There's only two of us left for the whole town. We're killing ourselves. Two's not enough.

GEORGE: I'm sorry . . .

On Thomas.

DR THOMAS: You'd be working as a doctor, George. And there'd be no one to order you around. You wouldn't be working in the hospital. We'd give you the dock area.

GEORGE: No, Thomas. Go away. It's still much too easy.

DR THOMAS: Think about it George, please. I'll send a car for you in half an hour. I beg you, give it some thought.

GEORGE: Goodbye, Thomas.

DR THOMAS: See you soon.

Thomas goes out.

Thomas outside. He takes his motorcycle, which he had leaned up against the cabin, and goes down to the road, pushing it beside him. He starts it up and sets off for the town. He passes a car coming in the opposite direction. Smoke is pouring from its radiator and it comes to a halt. Thomas is already a long way off. An irritable Starrett gets out of the car and lifts the bonnet. Smoke.

He stands up straight, looks around, sees George's cabin and sets off towards it.

Exterior of George's cabin. Starrett knocks and enters.

Interior of the cabin. Starrett, Nellie and George.

On George. He is looking at Starrett.

George and Starrett.

On Starrett.

On George.
Starrett and George.

DR STARRETT: The bloody thing!

Do you have any water? My radiator's run dry.

GEORGE: Take some from the barrel.

You're not a doctor, are you?

DR STARRETT: What's that to you?

GEORGE (*softly*): Don't do it, my friend. Don't do it.

DR STARRETT: What do you mean? What are you talking about?

GEORGE: You're clearing off, aren't you?

DR STARRETT: Who are you? Who told you?

GEORGE: Nobody told me. But I recognize the way you look, these twitches

He makes for the door.

George takes him by the shoulders.

and your hunted look. *I* was the same. That was six years ago.

DR STARRETT: Let me by.

GEORGE: I won't tell you there are thousands of lives to be saved. I imagine you've already thought of that. And it didn't stop you. But *for you*, for your self, you're making a terrible blunder.

DR STARRETT: Are you going to give me some water or not?

GEORGE: Take it if you want. The barrel's there. You'll find a bucket on the left.

Starrett pushes him away and goes to the back of the cabin. He takes the bucket. George follows him, stoops down and picks up his uniform from behind the table. He puts it on the table.

Look at that. That was mine. I used to wear it.

DR STARRETT: What's that to me?

GEORGE: I was posted to Colombo temporarily, to deal with an epidemic. It wasn't typhus—it was cholera. Two doctors out of seven died. I was six nights without sleep and then, one fine morning, I got into my car and drove as far away as I could. There you have it. And look what became of me. You don't get over it, I swear to you. Never. I've never been able to forget. You don't know how painful it's going to be. Oh, if only I could make you understand. If only I could teach you what I learned!

Starrett has gone and filled the bucket. He comes back over to George and looks at him.

DR STARRETT: Sleep's dead. Mountain and Thomas have kept the hospital for themselves because it's less dangerous. Do you know where they'll send me if I stay? The dock area. There's more than a hundred typhus patients there. I'll have to live among them and treat them round the clock. If you're a doctor, you can work out what chance I have of getting out of there.

GEORGE: One in a hundred or thereabouts. But I'd rather die than go through that again. If I had to start over . . .

Starrett comes back to the door with his bucket. He is extremely agitated.

He opens the door and goes out.

DR STARRETT: Yes, well I'm quite keen to live, thank you. Let me pass. Goodbye.

George and Nellie.

He opens the door. George, shot full-length from behind in the doorway. He describes what he is seeing.

He comes back to the table. He looks at his uniform. Nellie comes over to him and gives him a worried look.

He has straightened up and is smiling. He has a look of deliverance about him.

On Nellie.

GEORGE (*to himself*): If I had to start over . . .

He's putting water in the radiator. He's getting back in the car. He's going. That's me, Nellie. That's me leaving. Six years ago, with this same sun beating down . . . Poor sod.

NELLIE (*softly*): One chance in a hundred, George.

GEORGE: Yes, one chance in a hundred. Well!

NELLIE: What are you going to do?

GEORGE: Help me. I want to put my uniform on.

NELLIE: You're not going over there? You're not going to agree to that? You know how it is. They won't show you any gratitude. They're just using you because you're crazy—it's just to save the precious lives of the official doctors. And there's every chance it'll be the last thing you do.

On Nellie. She is gripped by violent anger.

She gives a nervous laugh.

George and Nellie. George views the uniform with a different look in his eyes. He touches it.

GEORGE (*softly*): That's what made my mind up for me.

NELLIE: Well, go on then. Go and die over there on your own. You have no heart any more. Your pride has turned you to stone.

How stupid I was. God, how stupid I was. I thought you'd try to start your life over . . .

GEORGE: Well, Nellie, I am starting it over.

NELLIE: Oh, I've heard enough. You're done for. You should have started again patiently, modestly, little by little. But you prefer a week of heroism with death at the end. That's easier, do you see? It's easier. What's difficult is being unassuming.

GEORGE: Nellie, I don't yet have the right to be unassuming. I'd always be afraid of having been a coward . . . We're dirty, Nellie. We have to wash ourselves.

Nellie comes over to him and puts her hands on his shoulders.

NELLIE: If you loved me . . .

George looks at her, troubled. He hesitates, about to take her in his arms. But he gathers himself and, with difficulty, says:

GEORGE: Who told you I loved you? I don't love you, Nellie. I don't love you.

Nellie gives a nervous laugh.

NELLIE: I . . . I wonder what I'm doing here, then.

She leans on the table as though she were going to fall. He wants to hold her, but she pulls away violently. She knocks the uniform off the table with the back of her hand, throwing it to the floor. Then she moves towards the door and exits.

George from behind. He staggers towards the door.

GEORGE: Nellie!

George from behind, framed in the doorway.

No answer. He comes back in slowly, reaches down with difficulty and picks up his uniform.

Nellie!

Shot of Nellie on the road. She is striding out, staring straight ahead, her hair flowing in the wind. A motor ambulance passes her, travelling in the opposite direction.

We follow the motor ambulance, which has just stopped at the roadside by George's cabin. The driver blows his horn (this is shot from below the cabin). Renewed blasts on the horn.

George appears in the doorway in his uniform. He is staggering somewhat, and walks down to the car with difficulty. With his bandages and his uniform, he has a rather crazed look, part alarming, part risible. As he is coming out, the car turns around and stops. George gets in beside the driver and the ambulance drives off.

View of Nellie, very small in the distance, through the windscreen. George sitting very stiffly beside the driver. Nellie grows larger and the car passes her. George remains stiff and silent. We can't tell whether he saw her. He doesn't turn around.

*

Nellie on the road. She comes into the town. We see her walking. Shot of Nellie from behind in a long street. Everywhere the windows are closed and the iron shutters on the shops are down.

There are tram rails down the middle of the street with an abandoned trailer on them (as in the first shots of the film).

She turns right into an alleyway and the camera follows her. A covered market, with its stalls deserted. There are fabrics, fruit and vegetables all over the floor (as in the first shots; the same set should be used). The streets and alleyways are absolutely empty. A pack of dogs runs across in front of Nellie. She is still walking. A skinned sheep on a butcher's stall.

The street the 'Mount Everest' is on. Nellie walking, shot in profile and then from behind. The bar door is open. She goes in. The bar is deserted and the chairs are on the tables. She goes behind the counter. Rikko is stretched out in the half-darkness at her feet. His body is stiff and his eyes stare blankly. Nellie looks at him for a moment, then runs off.

The square outside the Victoria Hotel. The hotel, with its shutters down and door closed, is at the back left. Nellie shot from behind, running up to the

The monotonous sound of Nellie's steps. Dogs barking in the distance.

hotel. She bangs on the door, using the hotel's door-knocker.

No answer.

She knocks harder, and for a long time, in a sort of fit of hysterics.

The camera pulls back. Nellie is still knocking. She looks very tiny in the enormous deserted square.

Dissolve.

Noise of hammering.

More violent knocking.

*   *

On the quayside. A large, open-sided shed beside the water. In the shed, natives are laid out beside each other in two rows. There is a narrow corridor running down the shed between the two rows. Not far away, behind this shed, we can see two very similar ones and can just make out other natives laid out in the same way. On the right, the deserted quayside and the empty dock. The camera will show the deserted docks and the cranes lying idle. Gulls in the sky.

On the left is a small brick house—the 'pavilion'. This is George's temporary home.

George and a (female) nurse in the shed. They are standing in the centre of the corridor between the rows of natives and are shot full-length, face to camera. Behind them is Rango, a Malay.

George is in uniform, bare-headed. He no longer has any bandages around his head and is clean shaven. A few scars on his face, a few bits of sticking-plaster above his eyes and at the corner of his mouth.

The nurse and George go over to a lifeless-looking Malay. George kneels down and raises the man's head. The nurse remains standing at his side.

Groans coming from all parts of the shed.

NURSE: That one's done for.

GEORGE (*curtly*): They're done for when they're dead. Not before. Pass me my bag.

He turns around, staggers and has to support himself by putting one hand to the ground.

NURSE: Aren't you going to get a bit of sleep? You've been on the go for four days solid now.

GEORGE: I'm not here to sleep.

As he speaks, George gives the Malay an injection in the arm.

He leans over the man. The nurse gives a few brief sobs behind him. She is trying to control her emotions.

George stands up and, taking her by the shoulders, casts her an affectionate glance.

NURSE: Excuse me. It's... it's nothing. And yet I *have* had some sleep.

GEORGE: You're exhausted, my dear. And you're running a temperature. Let me see your eyes. They're much too bright. Have you a headache?

NURSE: Yes, behind my eyes.

GEORGE: Go and lie down for a while. I'm going to telephone for a replacement.

NURSE (*worried*): I'm not ... er ... sick?

GEORGE: No, no, my dear. It's just that your strength is flagging. And when you're in that state, you can pick up anything. Rango! Give her your arm. Take her to her room.

The nurse staggers forward a few steps. Rango and the nurse go off. George moves swiftly to the other end of the shed, where a telephone has been installed against one of the posts supporting the roof. He picks up the receiver and dials a number.

Doctor Astor here. I'd like to speak to Doctor Thomas ... Yes, thank you ... Hello, Thomas. Look, the nurse here is absolutely worn out. I'm even a little bit worried about her. She's got a high temperature and pain behind the eyes . . . I don't know. It could very well be. At least that's how it begins. No. No ambulance. I'm responsible for my staff. I'll look after her.

Yes, all right. I've helped 10 or so to pull through. A lot of serious cases, yes. But if we can support their hearts . . . Only I do need someone. Send me a replacement as fast as you can. I'm relying on you.

Hello, Thomas. You don't have a Nellie Dixmier among your patients? No, I don't know what's become of her. Yes, please, if you would. Get someone to find out. I've had no news of her for four days. Yes, do everything you can. I . . . I feel like a murderer.

Bye. Don't forget. A nurse ASAP. The car's on its way? Fine.

Have you found her, then?

A Malay comes in at the the back of the shed and comes over to George.

He hangs up and turns to the Malay.

MALAY: No, doctor sir.

GEORGE: Have you looked everywhere? Have you been to my hut?

The Malay nods.

To the 'Mount Everest'?

George looks horribly worried.

He takes a few steps towards the pavilion.

George in profile.

MALAY: 'Mount Everest' closed. Rikko dead. Owner and Nogaro gone.

GEORGE: What about the hotel?

MALAY: Hotel closed.

GEORGE: All right, thank you.

Whispering in his ears against the background of the Malay lament.

NELLIE'S VOICE: If you loved me . . .

GEORGE'S VOICE: I don't love you, Nellie. I don't love you.

The Malayan song, followed by Nellie singing 'In the Night of his Pride' . . .

George moving more quickly. We feel he is anxious and can no longer bear his anxiety. He almost runs (shot from behind) to the pavilion. He goes in.

A car stops a few yards from the pavilion. A nurse gets out. We don't see her face. We see her *from behind* walking towards the pavilion.

George in the pavilion. A trestle bed and a table. He seems to be hesitating and battling internally. Then he goes over to the table, opens the drawer and takes out a bottle of whisky, which he unstoppers.

DRIVER (*leaning out of the car*): It's here. In the low building there.

The nurse in the doorway, shot from behind. Over her shoulder we see George, almost from behind, who is making to drink straight from the bottle. The nurse runs up and strikes him on the arm, knocking the botttle to the floor.

George turns around, furious.

Nellie and George in profile, face to face, shot from the waist up. They burst out laughing. George puts his arm around her shoulders.

NURSE (*fury in her voice*): Aren't you ashamed of yourself? I leave you alone for three days and you go straight back to the bottle?

GEORGE: Why don't you just mind your own business?

I'm pleased you've come, Nellie. I wanted . . . I wanted to tell you . . .

NELLIE: You wanted to tell me you loved me, eh? But you can't get the words out. You're still too proud just to admit it.

GEORGE (*laughing*): Just a few more days, Nellie. A few more days and you'll see how unassuming I'll be.

For the moment, you'd better go. Go and wait for me at the hospital.

He takes her in his arms. A pause

NELLIE: Whatever are you thinking of?

Notes

1 The lady refers here to her two sons, but this appears to be an error. On the next page of the manuscript, she meets her two *daughters*. [Trans.]

2 Sartre writes 'bidonville' lower case here. At other points, he capitalizes it. [Trans.]

3 Sartre seems to have wavered on this point: was it more natural for the Governor to be sitting or standing when the doctors and the police chief arrived? (A. E.-S.)

4 This is presumably a slip. Sartre meant to write 'the soldiers' or, perhaps, 'the Malayan soldiers'. (A. E.-S.)

5 Notebook 2 ends here. The last page has been torn out. It is quite possible that Sartre decided to remove it, cutting the scene that begins here for reasons of concision. In fact, Mercutio and Nogaro will soon inform George that they have cut him out of the deal: they have gone themselves to accost the Malays leaving the hospital. If our assumption is correct, then Sartre quite simply forgot to cross out the last two lines of the page. (A. E.-S.)